BUGS *of* BRITISH COLUMBIA

John Acorn

Illustrations by Ian Sheldon

The Publisher: Lone Pine Publishing

10145-81 Ave.	202A, 1110 Seymour St.
Edmonton, AB T6E 1W9	Vancouver, BC V6B 3N3
Canada	Canada

Website: http://www.lonepinepublishing.com

Canadian Cataloguing in Publication Data
Acorn, John, 1958–
    Bugs of British Columbia

    Includes bibliographical references and index.
    ISBN 1-55105-231-8

    1. Insects—British Columbia—Identification. I. Sheldon, Ian, 1971–
II. Title.
QL476.A362 2001   595.7'09711   C00-911322-3

Editorial Director: Nancy Foulds
Project Editor: Lee Craig
Production Manager: Jody Reekie
Layout & Production: Heather Markham, Arlana Anderson-Hale, Monica Triska
Book Design: Heather Markham, Robert Weidemann
Cover Design: Robert Weidemann
Cover Illustration: Ian Sheldon (Long-horned Beetle)
Illustration: Ian Sheldon
Photography: John Acorn

The following illustrations are used with the permission of Ian Sheldon © 2000 & 1999: p. 28; p. 30; pp. 33–37; pp. 39–41; pp. 43–57.

We acknowledge the financial support of the Government of Canada through the Book Publishing Industry Development Program (BPIDP) for our publishing activities.

PC: *04*

CONTENTS

DEDICATION

To the Cannings family, who have done so many great things to promote the wonders of British Columbia's "bugs."

ACKNOWLEDGEMENTS

Working on this book was a great pleasure, largely thanks to Ian Sheldon, whose superb paintings brought the bugs of B.C. to life. Ian worked from his own impressive knowledge of arthropods, as well as slides and specimens. Special thanks go to Felix Sperling, George Ball and Danny Shpeley of the University of Alberta's E.H. Strickland Entomological Museum for allowing us to borrow specimens for reference. Thanks are due to Rob Cannings, who graciously agreed to look over the manuscript for me. The following people also helped by reviewing text and responding to queries: Gary Anweiler, Brian Brown, Ed Fuller, Robert Holmberg, Reuben Kaufman, Dave Lawrie, David Maddison, Chris Schmidt, Ales Smetana, Terry Thormin and Daryl Williams. The staff of Lone Pine Publishing have been a pleasure to work with, and I would especially like to recognize Lee Craig, Nancy Foulds and Shane Kennedy for their contributions. Finally, I would like to thank Dena Stockburger for her loving support, Jesse Acorn for his three-year-old perspective on life and my parents for allowing me to be a bugster throughout my childhood—a phase that apparently hasn't yet ended for me.

| Pale Swallowtail p. 28 | Anise Swallowtail p. 29 | Cabbage White p. 30 | Clouded Sulphur p. 31 |

BUTTERFLIES

| Spring Azure p. 32 | Purplish Copper p. 33 | Pacific Fritillary p. 34 | Great Spangled Fritillary, p. 35 |

| Lorquin's Admiral p. 36 | Field Crescent p. 37 | Mourning Cloak p. 38 | Painted Lady p. 39 |

| Red Admiral p. 40 | Common Wood Nymph, p. 41 | Monarch p. 42 | Polyphemus Moth, p. 43 |

MOTHS

| California Silk Moth, p. 44 | Hera Buck Moth p. 45 | Sheep Moth p. 46 | Great Ash Sphinx p. 47 |

Big Poplar
Sphinx, p. 48

Snowberry
Clearwing, p. 49

Garden Tiger
Moth, p. 50

Carpenterworm
Moth, p. 51

Hornet Moth
p. 52

MOTHS

California Tent
Caterpillar Moth, p. 53

Black Witch
p. 54

White Underwing
p. 55

Aholibah
Underwing, p. 56

Spear-Marked
Black, p. 57

Pacific Tiger
Beetle, p. 58

Primitive Tiger
Beetle, p. 59

Snail-Killer Carabid
p. 60

Fiery Hunter
p. 61

BEETLES

Big Dingy Ground
Beetle, p. 62

Burying Beetle
p. 63

Hairy Rove Beetle
p. 64

May Beetle
p. 65

Ten-Lined June
Beetle, p. 66

Golden Jewel
Beetle, p. 67

Pink-Faced Jewel
Beetle, p. 68

Western Eyed Click
Beetle, p. 69

Beer Beetle
p. 70

Southern Ladybug
p. 71

Two-Spot Ladybug
p. 72

Thirteen-Spot
Ladybug, p. 73

Spruce Sawyer
p. 74

California Prionus
p. 75

Banded Laurel
Borer, p. 76

Blue Milkweed
Beetle, p. 77

Wood Ant
p. 78

Carpenter Ant
p. 79

Bumblebee
p. 80

Blue Horntail
p. 81

WASPS, ANTS, BEES & SAWFLIES

Bald-Faced Hornet
p. 82

Yellow Jacket
p. 83

Paper Wasp
p. 84

Stump Stabber
p. 85

Thread-Waisted
Wasp, p. 86

Spider Wasp
p. 87

Hover Fly
p. 88

Horse Fly
p. 89

TWO-WINGED FLIES

Beeish Robber Fly
p. 90

Giant Crane Fly
p. 91

Sand Dune Bee Fly
p. 92

Snow Cranefly
p. 93

TWO-WINGED FLIES

Green Lacewing
p. 94

Snakefly
p. 95

Snow Scorpionfly
p. 96

Lace Bug
p. 97

LACEWINGS, SNAKEFLIES & THE LIKE

SUCKING BUGS

Western Boxelder
Bug, p. 98

Rough Plant Bug
p. 99

Ambush Bug
p. 100

Western Okanagan
Cicada, p. 101

Northern Rock
Crawler, p. 102

Field Cricket
p. 103

Cave Cricket
p. 104

Primitive Monster
Cricket, p. 105

GRIGS

Red-Winged
Clickhopper, p. 106

European Earwig
p. 107

Minor Ground Mantid
p. 108

Giant Stonefly
p. 109

EARWIGS & OTHERS

Pacific Dampwood
Termite, p. 110

German Cockroach
p. 111

Boreal Bluet
p. 112

Pacific Forktail
p. 113

DRAGONFLIES & DAMSELFLIES

Common
Spreadwing, p. 114

Blue-Eyed Darner
p. 115

Pale Snaketail
p. 116

American Emerald
p. 117

Hudsonian
Whiteface, p. 118

Four-Spotted Skimmer
p. 119

Cherry-Faced
Meadowhawk, p. 120

Black Meadowhawk
p. 121

Snow Flea
p. 122

Kayak Pond
Skater, p. 123

Giant Water Bug
p. 124

Water Boatman
p. 125

Common
Backswimmer, p. 126

SPRINGTAILS   AQUATIC ADULTS

Acilius Diving
Beetle, p. 127

Water Scorpion
p. 128

Giant Diving
Beetles, p. 129

Whirligig Beetle
p. 130

Giant Water Scavenger
Beetle, p. 131

Damselfly Larva
p. 132

Dragonfly Larva
p. 133

Water Tiger
p. 134

Caddisfly Larva
p. 135

Giant Stonefly Larva
p. 136

AQUATIC LARVAE

Mayfly Larva
p. 137

Sow Bug
p. 138

Garden Centipede
p. 139

Cyanide Millipede
p. 140

NON-INSECT ARTHROPODS

Northern Scorpion
p. 141

Northern Camel
Spider, p. 142

Harvestman
p. 143

Rocky Mountain
Wood Tick, p. 144

Wolf Spider
p. 145

Boreal Jumping
Spider, p. 146

Orb-Weaver
p. 147

Long-Jawed Orb-
Weaver, p. 148

Giant House
Spider, p. 149

Six-Spotted Fishing
Spider, p. 150

Western Black
Widow, p. 151

Goldenrod Crab
Spider, p. 152

INTRODUCTION

This book is for bugsters. If you haven't heard the term, don't feel left out. I think I invented it with the help of my friends. We needed a word for people who are fascinated by insects, and enjoy them for no other reason than their intrinsic niftiness. "Amateur entomologist" seemed too stuffy, as did "insect enthusiast" and "entomophile." "Bugger" is out of the question. So are "bug-nut" and "bug-lover," mostly because they sound too silly. I did find the term "entomaniac" popular among some of the people I know, but it probably isn't the best one to use as a recruiting tool. Maniacs are crazy, but we bugsters are merely enthusiastic.

Even the word "bug" is fraught with problems. In the strict language of entomology, a bug is a member of the Order Hemiptera, often pedantically called "true bugs," although I prefer the more neutral "sucking bugs" myself, in reference to their sucking, not chewing, mouthparts. All other insects, including true bugs, are simply "insects." In technical language, when one expands the scope to include spiders, centipedes and millipedes, one has to resort to the phrase "terrestrial arthropods." It's tough to say that without sounding pretentious. So let's just cut through all of this confusion, and call the critters bugs, and the people who love them bugsters. It works for me, and the only reason it was difficult to arrive at, is that our language simply hasn't been called upon to develop everyday words to go with these ideas.

The lack of an everyday vocabulary is odd, given the enduring appeal of bugs. Some, like butterflies, are beautiful. Others, like ladybugs and bumblebees, are familiar personalities in the garden. Then there are those that are fascinating in a scary sort of way, such as spiders and scorpions. On top of all this, there is the wonderful diversity of insect life, and the delight that is generated by such a wide variety of living forms "right under our noses." Biologists these days like to call this wide variety "biodiversity," and there are some who claim that people are naturally predisposed to appreciate and crave contact with it. This idea, in turn, is called "biophilia," which can be translated as "the love of living things." I am not so sure that I agree with the biophilia hypothesis, because there are so many people out there who couldn't care less about the world of plants and animals. For those who feel the connection, however, the idea of "biophilia" can be a great comfort.

Of course, not all bugs are beneficial to people, and every single one of them is smaller than a hamster. Hence, as a society, we have developed a rather disdainful attitude toward bugs. As a consequence, most of the people who have done things to improve our understanding and appreciation of bugs have been professional biologists. Of these, entomologists study insects, while arachnologists study arachnids. Those scientists who study other sorts of bugs are generally called invertebrate zoologists, and this term can also be used to refer to the whole gang at once.

In British Columbia, the tradition of bug study has gone on primarily in the universities, as well as in research facilities operated by both the provincial and federal governments. Forest and crop pests have attracted their share of attention, as have biting flies and other bugs of medical or veterinary importance. Yet there have been some professional bugsters who have studied their subjects out of "pure" fascination, and there have also been many talented and devoted amateurs who have contributed to the knowledge of B.C.'s bugs as well.

We seem poised for a resurgence of interest in our arthropod neighbours, what with a proliferation of bug-related movies, children's books and toys in the last few years. I suppose this book will probably be considered part of the same "craze," but I hope it will survive beyond that. For this reason, I have tried to make the book as entomologically correct as I could muster, while still retaining a spirit of fun and informality. Having actively participated in the dinosaur craze of the 1980s, it seems to me that after the wave has passed, what we are left with is the fact that the subject is still

interesting. As well, the interesting things about it are still generated by the core group of people who cared about it before the fad, and will continue to care in the future.

There are about 20,000 species of bugs in B.C. This number is a guess, of course, and the reason we don't know exactly is that there are still new species waiting to be discovered by science, and there are many species known elsewhere that are waiting to be found here in B.C. Choosing the 125 "coolest" species was a challenge for me. I tried to pick bugs that are either

1) **big,**
2) **colourful,**
3) **really hard to miss or**
4) **extremely weird.**

The point of this book is to introduce you to the bugs of B.C., not to serve as a guide to the whole kit and caboodle (whatever a "caboodle" might be). I hope you realize that to a hard-core bugster like myself, every single one of those 20,000 species has the potential to be wonderfully interesting in its own right. In other words, this book is supposed to be inspiring more than scholastic.

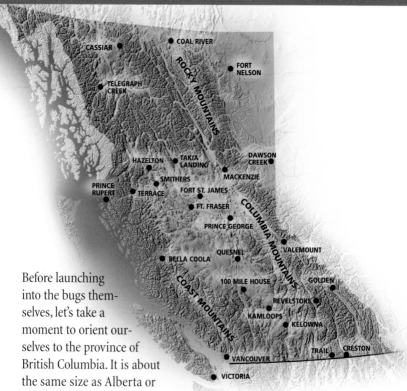

Before launching into the bugs themselves, let's take a moment to orient ourselves to the province of British Columbia. It is about the same size as Alberta or Saskatchewan, taller than it is wide, with straight-line borders at its north and south ends. The eastern border follows the continental divide in the southern half of the province and the 120th line of longitude in the north, forming a distinct angle where they meet. On the west side, the province is bordered by the Pacific Ocean, and it includes a number of islands, the largest of which is Vancouver Island, where Victoria, the provincial capital, is located. For the most part, B.C. is a mountainous place, its two main ranges being the Rockies in the east and the Coast Mountains in the west. In between lies "the Interior," a land of lower mountains, plateaus and valleys, the best-known part of which is called the Okanagan. A few other small mountain ranges pop up in the southeast, notably the Selkirks, Purcells and Monashees (collectively, the Columbia Mountains). The northeastern corner of the province is much like the boreal forest to the east, and it is the coldest part of the province by far. The coastal regions are generally quite warm and moist, receiving much rainfall, and the interior is much drier—in summer, the Okanagan is almost desert-like. By Canadian standards, B.C. is a relatively warm, lush place to live, although winter rains in Vancouver can be incessant, and summer heat in the Okanagan can be oppressive. Still, it is a naturalist's paradise and a bugster's dream.

BASIC BUG BANTER

Like any science, the study of bugs has its own jargon. Some of its words have plain-language equivalents, but others do not. Unavoidably, then, it is important to get the gist of things before going on to read more about the bugs themselves. I suppose I could have presented this section as a glossary, but I think it will be more interesting as a sort of condensed textbook. I hope you agree.

Bug Structure

Let's start with the structure, or anatomy, of bugs, and let's also start at the front end of an average adult specimen. They all have a head, and on the head there are almost always eyes (with either one lens or many), a mouth, a set of appendages called **mouthparts** and a pair of feelers called **antennae** (one is an antenna). Eyes with multiple lenses are called **compound eyes**; eyes with one lens are called **ocelli** (one is an ocellus).

On many bugs the head is joined to the rest of the body by an obvious line or groove, and it is somewhat moveable on a flexible but very short neck.

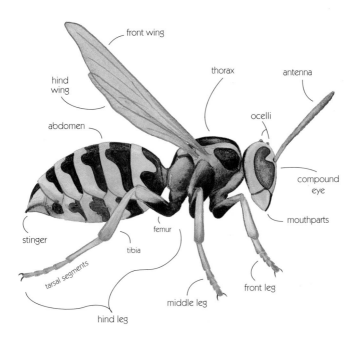

front wing

thorax

antenna

hind wing

ocelli

abdomen

compound eye

mouthparts

stinger

femur

tibia

front leg

tarsal segments

middle leg

hind leg

In others (spiders and scorpions, for example), the head is part-and-parcel of a larger body part—the **cephalothorax**—that also bears the legs. Major body parts, which is to say the head, thorax, cephalothorax or abdomen, are often further divided into segments, and the segments may or may not be easy to recognize on the surface.

Insects have a separate **thorax**, which is easy to recognize because it is the part of the body that bears the legs. The thorax is in turn divided into three segments, each of which bears a single pair of legs. If wings are present, the two pairs are borne by the middle and hind segments. In many groups, the front wings are thickened and serve as wing-covers for the hind wings. The three segments that make up the thorax are called the **prothorax**, **mesothorax** and **metathorax**. On beetles, the only part of the thorax that is visible from above is the prothorax, the top of which is called the pronotum.

Everything past the thorax is called the **abdomen**. At the tip of the abdomen, one finds the anus, the reproductive structures and, in many types of bugs, a rear-facing set of "feelers" called cerci (one is a cercus).

There are few other obvious aspects to the anatomy of a bug, but they include **spiracles** on the sides of the thorax and abdomen (openings for the multi-branched breathing tubes of insects, called the tracheal system) or book lung openings on the underside of spiders, near the silk-producing **spinnerets**. Some aquatic insects (insects that live in the water) have **gills** as well, most of which are leafy or finely branched projections from the body. Scorpions have comb-like sensory appendages on the underside of their cephalothorax called **pectines**.

Life History

Now let's discuss life history. Most bugs begin life as an egg. The egg then hatches into a baby bug, but not all baby bugs look like their parents.

Larva   *Pupa*   *Larva*

| *Pupa* | *Larva* | *Naiad* |

Generally, if the newly hatched young look more-or-less like the adults (baby grasshoppers, for example), they are likely to be called **nymphs**. If the young are clearly different from the adults, the word **larva** is more widely used (although the larvae of butterflies and moths are called caterpillars). Some aquatic nymphs are called **naiads**, and spider babies are simply **spiderlings**. Entomologists have recently agreed to use the word "larvae" to refer to all sorts of immature insects, but they have to fight a long history of confusion to do so. If you think this is complicated, compare it to the situation with mammals, where you have to distinguish among pups, kids, calves, kits, foals, colts, lambs and so on.

As bugs grow, they have to shed their outer covering, which is called the **exoskeleton** (or more properly, the exocuticle), numerous times. Some simply increase in size until they are large enough and mature enough to reproduce. Others show more obvious changes as they grow, the most common of which is the development of wings and genitalia. The genitalia are the sexual parts of bugs, and they are often complicated, involving hooks and claspers, as well as things that look like levers, pliers, syringes and the like. Sometimes they are visible from the outside and sometimes not. In spiders, one pair of mouthparts serve as the male sex organs (the pedipalps), and in dragonflies and damselflies the males have one set of genitalia at the tip of the abdomen and another at the base. (The base of a structure, by the way, is always the place where it attaches to the rest of the body.)

When a bug reaches the full-grown, ready-to-reproduce state, it is simply called an adult. However, in order for caterpillars and other grub-like larvae to become adults, they first have to enter into a resting stage, called the **pupa** (the plural is pupae), during which the amazing transformation takes place. Butterfly pupae are sometimes called **chrysalids**, and remember that the silk covering that some caterpillars make when they pupate, and not the pupa itself, is called a **cocoon**.

The change from young to adult is called **metamorphosis**, and there are three sorts. If the change is gradual, what we have is "gradual metamorphosis." If it involves the development of wings, or some other fairly major change in body form, it is called "incomplete metamorphosis." If it involves a pupal stage, it is called "complete metamorphosis." These terms are old-fashioned and, of course, there is nothing defective about an insect with "incomplete metamorphosis."

Ecology

The ecology of bugs has to do with how they interact with other living things and with their non-living environment. The place where an insect lives is called its **habitat**, a word that means about the same as environment. All of the plants and animals in a given habitat are called a **community**, and even larger such groupings are called **ecosystems**. An insect may recognize its habitat by soil type, by slope (or flatness), by altitude, by water characteristics (flow speed, dissolved oxygen, temperature and so on) or by the presence of specific types of prey or species of plants. If an insect eats plants, the plants are called host plants or food plants, and the insects are called **herbivores**. If an insect drinks nectar, the plants are called **nectar plants**. Insects that eat other creatures are **predators**, while the creatures they eat are **prey**. If an insect lives on or inside a host animal, and either kills it very slowly or not at all, it is called a **parasite**. If it is a parasite only in the larval stage, and it eventually kills its host, it is called a **parasitoid**. If an insect eats things that are already dead, it is called a **scavenger**. If it eats poop, it is said to be **coprophagous**. Complex, isn't it? Also remember that movement of insects in one direction is called **dispersal**, while two-way movement with the seasons is called **migration**.

There, that should do it for ecology. Now on to systematics.

Bug Systematics

Systematics is the study of how living things are related, in an evolutionary sense. In order to reconstruct the evolutionary tree of life, you really have to start with the basic unit of evolutionary change, the species. Species are groups of living things that can interbreed in nature without hybridizing ("crossing") with other species—at least not *too* much. Species are grouped with other closely related species into genera, the singular of which is genus. Genera are grouped into families, families into orders, orders into classes and classes into phyla. This system is called the Linnaean system of classification. The singular of phyla is phylum, and all of the critters in this book belong to one phylum, the Arthropoda or "joint-legged animals." These are what I call "bugs."

Within the phylum Arthropoda, I have chosen examples from five classes: the crustaceans (Class Crustacea), the millipedes (Class Diplopoda), the centipedes (Class Chilopoda), the arachnids (Class Arachnida) and the insects (Class Insecta). The arachnids are further divided into five orders in this book: the spiders (Order Aranaea), the harvestmen (Order Opiliones), the scorpions (Order Scorpionida), the camel spiders (Order Solifugae) and the mites and ticks (Order Acarina).

Because of their great diversity, the situation with the insects is a bit more complex (and there are a number of classification schemes as well, so don't be surprised if not all bug books use the same names I use here). Beginning with the flightless insects, we start with springtails, in the Order Collembola. These insects show gradual metamorphosis. Then we come to the insects with wings and incomplete metamorphosis, beginning with the dragonflies and damselflies, in the Order Odonata, the mayflies in the Order Ephemeroptera and the stoneflies in the Order Plecoptera. Next come the grasshoppers, crickets and such (the grigs, as some people call them) in the Order Orthoptera and the cockroaches in the Order Dictyoptera. Sucking bugs (the so-called true bugs) also fall into this part of the classification, and they form the Order Hemiptera.

The rest of the insects have complete metamorphosis, with a pupa stage. They include the two-winged flies (the "true flies") in the Order Diptera, the wasps, bees and ants in the Order Hymenoptera, the beetles in the Order Coleoptera, the caddisflies in the Order Trichoptera, the lacewings and ant-lions in the Order Neuroptera and the butterflies and moths in the Order Lepidoptera.

By the way, the root "ptera" refers to wings, Hemiptera means half-wing, Diptera means two-wing, Lepidoptera means scaly-wing and so on. If you look into the meanings of scientific names, it will help you remember them, but really there is no

"Eyeball" Orb-weaver

substitute for simply memorizing the words and getting on with the more interesting aspects of entomology. Note as well that one species is abbreviated as "sp." and many species as "spp."

In most bug books, the various groups are presented in the order that I have just given. This places closely related groups together, and begins with those bugs that are most primitive (in the sense of resembling the long-extinct common ancestor of the entire group) and ends with those that are most derived (a term that means they have undergone a great deal of evolutionary change). In this book, however, I have chosen to reverse the order. This order still keeps related species together, and gives you all the insight that the traditional order does, but it also allows you to start with butterflies and moths, rather than springtails. Because my goal is to get you to like these animals, I chose to begin with the niftiest ones. At the end of the insects, however, I have "artificially" grouped a number of unrelated aquatic insects together in one section. After all, that is the way many entomologists think of them—as a unit. The non-insects follow the aquatic insects.

BEING A BUGSTER

This is not a book about pests and how to kill them. Sure, some bugs are harmful, and I don't object to fighting back when the need arises, so long as no other species, or people, are caught in the crossfire. In fact, you'll find that some of my favourite bugs are pests. After all, it is always possible to admire the positive qualities of your enemies, even in the heat of battle.

Most bugs, however, are harmless, and all good bugsters know that they are the very backbone of the ecology of B.C., responsible for everything from pollination to decomposition, soil formation, regulation of other bugs and "weeds," food for birds and mammals, and so on. Without apology, I think that all bugs are worthy of admiration and respect and at least a passing glance. If you don't understand bugs, you really don't understand the world in which you live.

Bugs are easy to find, at least on warm days during bug season, which means roughly late March through October. This season leaves us with only four months in which bugs are hard to find, which in my opinion is pretty darn good. Of course, May through September is the best time for bugs, during which they are downright hard to miss. Bugs live in almost every conceivable habitat, from the alpine tundra on the tops of the highest mountains to the driest prairie sand dune, the insides of caves, the insides of our homes and every place in between.

The author and his son, bug watching

Still, if you want to go out searching for bugs, I suggest looking for them in habitats such as these:

1) under rocks and boards (and remember to put the rocks and boards back once you look),
2) on plants, and especially on flowers and the undersides of leaves,
3) at lights at night (but not the yellow bug-free lights),
4) in the water, especially where there are lots of water plants,
5) on bare sandy ground, even if it is far from water, and
6) at various sorts of "bait."

My favourite bug baits include various mixtures of beer and sugar, painted on trees for moths and butterflies, as well as less appealing things such as dung and carrion. Don't feel bad if you choose to ignore the bug-baiting option—after all, many sorts of bait are downright unhygienic. Remember not to touch the bait, and always wash your hands afterwards—something my mother used to tell me often when I was a junior entomaniac.

In general, bugs like warm weather more than cool, and they are easier to find in sunny places than in the shade. They prefer humid days to dry, but they don't do much in the rain. Warm nights will bring out many flying insects, such as moths, while cool ones will not. During a full moon, bugs are less attracted to lights. Wind does not necessarily deter bug activity, but it

A Nikon 5T lens on a pair of binoculars

certainly makes them harder to find and to follow. Daytime bugs get going at about 9 a.m., and they slow down appreciably by around 7 p.m., at least during mid-summer.

The easiest way to get a close look at a bug is to catch it, examine it, and let it go. Nets are easy to make, and good ones are also inexpensive to buy through mail-order. Small bugs can be placed in clean jars for a brief period, while large ones, such as butterflies and dragonflies, can be gently examined while still in the net. Many bugs can gently be handled. In my opinion, this is the overall best way to approach the study of bugs, and it gives a great deal of satisfaction for very little effort. All of the suggestions that follow involve more work, and more of a commitment to mastering unusual techniques.

If you want to watch bugs without disturbing them, you can do it the old-fashioned way, on your elbows with a Sherlock Holmes magnifying glass, or you can try other sorts of optical tools. I recommend the Bushnell close-focusing 8-power monocular, model 14-8200 (it focuses to a distance of about 20 cm and costs less than $50, although I have heard that it will soon be out of production). You might also try a pair of compact binoculars, such as the Bushnell Natureview 8 X 30, with a Nikon 5T close-up lens held in front of it (total cost about $200–250). You get a clear view of the bug, at a distance of about half a metre, with both eyes at once.

Depending on what sort of bug you choose to watch, your style will have to be modified. When I watch tiger beetles, I find myself crawling around on the sand, continually moving to follow my subjects. On the other hand, I often place a small folding chair in front of a buggy-looking plant, and then sit in one place while scanning the flowers, leaves and stems for interesting creatures on which to spy.

There is much to learn from bug watching. Since the behaviour of many of our local bugs is poorly known, any of us has the ability to make useful observations once we have learned to identify the creatures we are encountering. On the other hand, simply immersing yourself in the lives of insects and other buggy critters is a wonderful way to make a deep and moving connection with the non-human world all around us. You can be as scientific or as recreational as you want.

If you make detailed observations of particular sorts of insect, it is probably a good idea to collect a few "voucher specimens," so other bugsters can confirm your identifications later (for easy-to-identify species, a close-up photograph will also suffice). When I was young, the *only* way to approach bug study was to make a collection. Collecting is still allowed, almost anywhere except in national and provincial parks, but it is no longer a popular activity.

If you choose to make a collection for educational or scientific reasons, remember to limit your catch, treat every specimen with respect, take the time to label, arrange, and store the specimens correctly, and plan to donate them to a university or museum once you are done with them. Instructions for insect collecting are easy to come by, and for the most part you will only encounter ill-will when you collect and kill butterflies and moths—most people feel little sympathy for other sorts of bugs.

Increasingly, however, bugsters are polarizing into collecting

and anti-collecting camps. I wish they weren't, but because they are, I want to briefly discuss the matter. Collectors claim they do not harm bug populations—bugs generally have short generation times and high reproduction rates, and they recover from "harvest" much more easily than vertebrates. Collectors also point out that the identities of pinned

Danny Shpeley, with a research collection

specimens can be confirmed, whereas sightings are always subject to doubt. Anti-collectors, on the other hand, are reluctant to admit that bug collecting is always innocent, because it *must* be possible for a large enough group of collectors to cause local extinctions of small, isolated "colonies" of rare bugs. These are exactly the sorts of bugs that collectors seek, so this fear could be well-founded if collecting were ever to become truly popular (which in itself seems unlikely). Unfortunately, these isolated populations also become places where collectors and anti-collectors come into uncomfortable proximity with one another, at which point it is very difficult for the watchers to do their thing with collectors chasing the very bugs they want to observe, and *vice versa*.

When I try my hardest to be rational about this subject, it seems obvious to me that insect collectors are not a big threat to the insects of British Columbia. In fact, I believe they are inconsequential. Logging, pesticides and habitat destruction are all of much greater concern. It seems to me that the real core of the collector/anti-collector debate has to do with two rather unscientific human motives. First, no one likes having their freedom (or the freedom of their favourite bugs) restricted, especially when no laws exist to back the restrictions up. Second, collectors and anti-collectors seem to dislike the sorts of people that each other represents. On the one hand, let's admit that it is difficult to sympathize with those who kill the very objects of their passion. On the other, it is difficult to take people's scientific motives seriously when they are willfully unsure of the identities of the creatures they are observing and could easily remedy the situation by catching a few. It also seems clear to me that peer pressure has a great deal to do with the attitudes of individual bugsters—in a group of watchers, no one dares bring out a net; among collectors, the binoculars stay in their cases.

As for my personal approach, I usually go out with nothing but binoculars and a camera, content to watch and admire. When I'm doing

Winter water bugsters: Chris Fisher and John Acorn

something scientific, I also take a net. I sometimes collect a specimen or two, but most of the time I use institutional collections for research. I still find many uses for pinned insects (for example, when writing this book), but I no longer feel a deep-seated need to possess them for myself. I try to act respectfully toward bugs whenever I can, but I'll admit that it is difficult to avoid inconsistency when swatting mosquitoes or splattering bugs on a windshield one moment, then treating bugs like endangered panda bears the next. The way I see it, this sort of "hypocrisy" is inescapable, and one can use it to either justify a callous attitude toward bugs, or accept it and atone by acting kindly toward them whenever possible.

Another fascinating bugster activity is insect rearing, which is much less controversial than collecting or watching, because people who rear bugs are more-or-less forced to treat them with loving care, and they will inevitably acquire a specimen or two through accidental mortality. Most often, when people want to rear bugs, they start with some caterpillars and wait to see what type of butterfly or moth they will turn into. To rear caterpillars, put them in a well-ventilated cage and provide them with plenty of leaves to eat. Place the cut stems in water with some means of preventing the caterpillars from drowning in the water supply (I place soft foam around the stems). When they are ready, some caterpillars pupate above ground, but for those that dig into the soil, make sure they have some potting soil or peat to dig in when the time comes. Then place the pupae in the refrigerator for winter, and mist them with water every few days, because refrigerators are terribly dry places. Rearing caterpillars is not easy—as they grow they require more and more fresh food, and their quarters need to be cleaned frequently. If you have a lot of them, they can be almost as much effort as a new puppy!

For other insects, you will have to be more creative with your rearing techniques, but there is more information available on this subject all the time. Temperature, humidity, food, light and making things escape-proof are all subjects you will have to consider carefully with each new species that you try. Another popular thing to do is to set up a pond aquarium, much the same way as setting up a tropical fish tank, but without a heater.

And remember, if your bugs don't look healthy, take them back to where you caught them, and let them go.

Of course, you should not forget the potential of bug photography or even bug drawing. These activities require specialized equipment, and a certain amount of practice, but there are plenty of good books on the market that can help you. With more and more sophisticated photo equipment available all the time, professional-quality bug photography is now possible with everyday equipment that you buy at an average camera store.

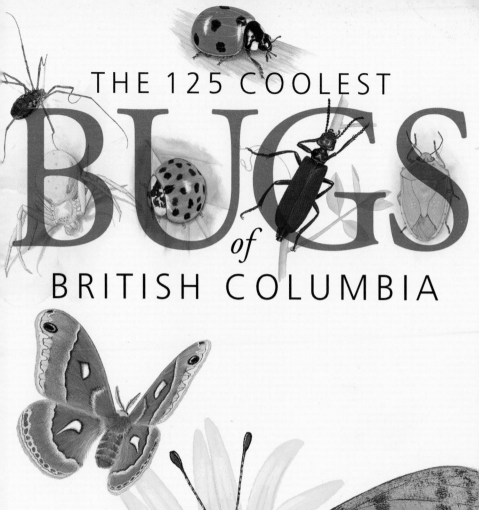

THE 125 COOLEST
BUGS
of
BRITISH COLUMBIA

PALE SWALLOWTAIL
Papilio eurymedon

$\mathbf{P}$ ale Swallowtails aren't really pale; they are white. Or, more accurately, they are creamy white and black. Because their close relatives in the tiger swallowtail group are all yellow and black, some people consider them "pale" by comparison, which really isn't fair. These big, bright butterflies are downright elegant, with a soaring flight style and graceful lines. While they sip at a flower, they nervously tremble their wings and dance on slender, black legs. They can flutter as lazily as any butterfly, or they can "put it in gear" and fly amazingly fast, with powerful, athletic wingbeats.

WINGSPAN: about 85 mm.
HABITAT: hilltops and clearings.

The Pale Swallowtail is easy to differentiate from the Western Tiger Swallowtail (*P. rutulus*) and the Two-tailed Swallowtail (*P. multicaudatus*), not only by colour but by its wide, dark wing borders as well. More than any other swallowtail, the Pale Swallowtail is characteristic of the West, and its range extends well into the Interior. This butterfly is a hill-topping one that prefers the high ground and also seems to like dry areas more than wet ones. The host plants for its caterpillars are all in the buckthorn family, and the caterpillars are typical for tiger-type swallowtails: greenish, with a false snake-head pattern on the thorax.

ANISE SWALLOWTAIL
Papilio zelicaon

I f you could see them side by side, the differences between an Anise Swallowtail and any of the tiger-type swallowtails (the Pale, Western Tiger and Two-tailed swallowtails) would be obvious. In the field, however, as one flits quickly past, it is easy to confuse them. The Anise is usually smaller, and it has a lot more black in its wing pattern than any of the tigers. As well, note that the tigers all have a dark line through the middle of the hind wing—something the Anise Swallowtail lacks. The Anise is a close relative of Europe's most common swallowtail, which is simply called the "Swallowtail" there and the "Old World Swallowtail" where it occurs in North America.

The Anise Swallowtail gets its name from a common food plant of its caterpillars, although they will also eat related plants, such as cow

WINGSPAN: about 70 mm.
HABITAT: hilltops and clearings.

parsnip and parsley. This butterfly is also one of the few with an attractive body: streamlined and luxuriantly furred in yellow and black. In fact, all of the swallowtails have elegant bodies. Even without their extravagant wings, they would be noteworthy bugs. And why do swallowtails have the "tails" on their hind wings? So that birds will grasp them, and fly away with a beak full of membrane, rather than the butterflies themselves.

CABBAGE WHITE
Pieris rapae

O ur least-loved butterfly is another European immigrant. Its caterpillars love nothing better than to drill through defenceless greens in a suburban vegetable garden. Europeans brought vegetables here from "the Old Country," and they brought this butterfly, too. For many people, this butterfly is the most familiar one of all, and it is certainly common in back alleys and other places where native species rarely venture. Up close, it is not a bad-looking creature, with subtle greens and yellows on a background of milky white.

The white colour was originally intended as a warning to birds that this butterfly tastes bad. However, because most of our Cabbage Whites grow up in gardens rather than among toxic wild weeds, they actually taste just fine. The similar Mustard White (*P. oleracea*) and Margined White (*P. marginalis*) live almost exclusively in natural areas and forests, where their caterpillars feed on wild members of the mustard family. Happily, it seems that the Cabbage White and its native relatives stay out of each other's way— the country whites and the city whites, so to speak.

WINGSPAN: 50 mm.
HABITAT: gardens and agricultural areas.

CLOUDED SULPHUR

Colias philodice

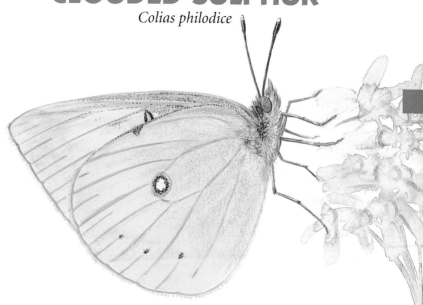

Sulphurs are so named because most of them are yellow. For this reason, they may also be responsible for the name "butter-fly." This derivation, of course, should be credited to the sulphurs that live in Europe, most of which are quite similar to our own. Over most of B.C., the Clouded Sulphur is by far the most common species, but identification can be a tricky chore where the others occur. In fact, some of the sulphurs are probably the toughest butterflies of all to identify correctly. Still, males of most of our species have solid black wing borders on the upper surface, while females have little, yellow spots within the black. Some sulphurs, despite the name, are orange.

Sulphurs are butterflies of open, sunny meadows and fields, as well as mountain tops and clearings. They have a direct, powerful style of flight

WINGSPAN: 50 mm.
HABITAT: widespread in open areas.

that really doesn't fit into the category of "fluttering." A great place to find Clouded Sulphurs is in an alfalfa field, where they sometimes fly in the thousands. The Clouded Sulphur goes through at least two generations during a typical butterfly season. The first to emerge are not the earliest butterflies of spring, but the last survivors are often the last butterflies in fall.

SPRING AZURE
Celastrina ladon

Bluebirds are fine for some, but for those people who love the smaller "blue" creatures, there is no more uplifting sight than the year's first Spring Azure. This lovely little butterfly, which flashes and dodges close to the ground, is as iridescent as a tropical parrot and as bright as the April skies above. Although other species of "blues" will appear later in the season, with darker blue colours and more crisply marked underwings, the Spring Azure is the one that comes out first, so this species is the one we know and love the best.

WINGSPAN: 25 mm.
HABITAT: widespread in forest clearings.

In fact, the Spring Azure is usually the first butterfly of the year to emerge from its pupa. Most of the other spring butterflies, such as Mourning Cloaks (p. 38) and Tortoise-shells, have spent winter as an adult butterfly, tucked away under bark or among deadfall. By the time late May rolls around, the last of the azures are looking grey and weather beaten. Most of them live only a week or two as adults, and their brief lives are usually squandered at the expense of their diminutive beauty. It is the males we see most often, because they fly whenever the sun is out, searching for females.

PURPLISH COPPER
Lycaena helloides

Anyone who takes an interest in butterflies will soon find that the subject is inexhaustible—just when you think you have encountered all of the butterfly types in your area, you notice a small, inconspicuous one, low to the ground. Most of the time, this butterfly will be a copper, and what a delight it is. B.C. coppers are usually at least partly orange, and a combination of orange-and-brown markings does give them a semi-coppery look. Of course, butterfly names aren't always accurate; a copper-coloured beetle is much more copper-coloured than these types of butterflies! Hey, how's that for confusing?

WINGSPAN: 25 mm.
HABITAT: widespread in open areas and clearings, especially moist ones.

The most common species of copper in B.C. is probably the Purplish Copper, of which only the males have a purple iridescence. Purplish Coppers first appear in late June or July, and in a warm year they can also have a second generation that emerges in September. It is this second generation that can be really abundant, spreading into suburban neighbourhoods and sipping at the blossoms of that ever-available butterfly-flower, the good old dandelion.

PACIFIC FRITILLARY
Boloria epithore

"Fritillary" is a confusing word. It refers to a large assortment of orange-and-black butterflies, and it can be pronounced either "FRIT-ill-erry" or "frit-TILL-err-ee." To make things more complicated, there are also flowers called fritillaries, and in Europe all sorts of semi-related butterflies are called fritillaries. The Pacific Fritillary is one of the so-called "lesser fritillaries," which are generally smaller than the greater fritillaries. As well, few of the lesser fritillaries have silver spots on their underwings.

WINGSPAN: about 37 mm.
HABITAT: widespread in meadows and clearings.

A number of species of lesser fritillaries emerge throughout the butterfly season, and they are easy to find because most of them have the enchanting habit of feeding while spreading their wings wide open to the sun. For this reason, they make great subjects for nature photography. Some live in meadows in forested regions, while others range far into the alpine zone at the tops of mountains. To tell a Pacific Fritillary from the other lesser "frits," one has to memorize the exact pattern of splotches on the underside of the hind wing—a fairly standard thing to do once you become a "hard-core butterflier."

GREAT SPANGLED FRITILLARY

Speyeria cybele

This butterfly is the greatest of the greater fritillaries of B.C. On the upper side of the wings, greaters look much like the lesser fritillaries, but on the underside, most of them have a dazzling array of bright silver spots. Because butterflies see things differently than people—and much of what they see lies in the ultraviolet range—these spots are bright ultraviolet beacons to other fritillaries. At a distance, fritillaries attract one another with their appearance, but when they get close, they choose to communicate with perfumes instead. Sound familiar?

Fritillary caterpillars, by the way, feed on the leaves of violets, and they only come out at night. In mid-summer, when the air is filled with fritillaries but the violets have finished blooming, you wouldn't think there were enough violet leaves to go around.

WINGSPAN: 60 mm.
HABITAT: forest clearings in the Interior and the Peace River area.

For those bug enthusiasts who like identification challenges, the greater fritillaries fit the bill perfectly. There are many species in B.C., and some of them are so similar to one another that even experts can't seem to agree on what name to use. In fact, it is only the experts who fail to agree; the rest of us don't even try.

LORQUIN'S ADMIRAL
Liminitis lorquini

A large, black butterfly with a white band through the middle of both sets of wings pretty much has to be an admiral. The name "admiral," by the way, was originally "admirable," which makes good sense. Too bad it faded from use. The Lorquin's Admiral is a very typically western species, easy to recognize because of the orange suffusion on the tips of the front wings. Entomologists seem to love the word "suffusion," which implies a certain blurriness, and it's a word that often comes in handy when describing insect colours.

WINGSPAN: about 65 mm.
HABITAT: forest clearings in the south.

Lorquin's Admiral is typical of its group in that it is often found sunning on either the ground or vegetation. It is also a common sight on wet ground, where it sips for nutrients. Apparently, when butterflies feed on mud, they are primarily after sodium, because it is hard to get sodium from flower nectar alone. (Don't think, however, that flower nectar is simple sugar water—it's not.) As well, admirals will sometimes sip at the most disgusting of wet things, including dead animals, dung and places where people or other animals have recently urinated. It's a good thing they are beautiful, or we might have trouble overlooking these habits.

FIELD CRESCENT
Phyciodes campestris

Tiny, bright and proud—that's how I think of crescents. These butter-flies are small, but they fly with the grace and assurance of a majestic Monarch (p. 42). Sometimes, they even glide, which is quite a feat at their size. Crescents are the smallest members of the brush-footed butterfly family—named for their tiny, brush-like front legs. They walk on only four legs, although really, they don't walk much at all, and the front legs have vir-tually disappeared through the process of evolution. Their middle and hind legs serve perfectly well to hold the body steady when they are at rest. At least that's what we believe now; perhaps someone will find that the tiny front legs actually serve some other un-known purpose.

WINGSPAN: about 30 mm.
HABITAT: widespread in meadows and clearings.

Crescents like to perch on a sunlit leaf and spread their intricately pat-terned wings to the sky. You get a great look at their features, but don't think these crescents are easy to identify—there are a number of species of amaz-ingly similar crescents. Despite this difficulty, enjoy them. In mid-summer, these butterflies are some of the most common in B.C., and they are easiest to find if there is a shrub where they can perch.

MOURNING CLOAK

Nymphalis antiopa

The Mourning Cloak is a big, heavy-bodied, spectacular butterfly. You can hope to see one on almost any sunny day, even in winter, that the temperature rises above about 10° C. The adults emerge in late July, at which point they are at their most magnificent—maroon with yellow trim and blazing blue highlights and with a bark-coloured pattern on the underside. After feeding for a week or so, they go into a temporary dormancy, and then emerge to feed again in fall. When the snow comes, they tuck in under a chunk of bark, a shutter or a fallen log and hibernate. Sometimes they die during hibernation, and you find their remains when you clean out the attic or the woodpile.

WINGSPAN: 70 mm.
HABITAT: widespread in forested areas.

The first warm days of spring bring them back out of hiding, and that's when they mate and lay eggs. By the time June rolls around, there are still a few on the wing—worn and tattered, with white wing fringes instead of yellow. A Mourning Cloak can live a full year as an adult, which is almost a year longer than most other butterflies.

PAINTED LADY
Vanessa cardui

A lovely orange, black and white butterfly, swift on the wing and with a love for thistles—that's the Painted Lady. Often, I hear people say that butterflies used to be very common in the good old days, but now they have all but disappeared. Well, in some places that may be true, but usually these people are recalling a time when Painted Ladies arrived on migration. The migration is something that happens only once every 10 or so years.

The populations of these butterflies build up in the southern U.S. over the course of a decade, at which point they swarm up into Canada by the bazillions. No thistle is safe from the egg-laying females, and a northern

WINGSPAN: 55 mm.
HABITAT: widespread in a variety of open areas.

generation grows up over summer. These butterflies, however, don't realize that they should return south in fall, and they all die when winter arrives. Although we usually have to wait another 10 years to see them again in such quantities, a few of these butterflies are around every year. Sometimes the invasion goes on for two or three years at a time.

RED ADMIRAL
Vanessa atalanta

T he Red Admiral is a close cousin to the Painted Lady (p. 39). Like the Lady, the Red Admiral is a migratory butterfly, and it is only common every once in a while. Its caterpillars, however, unlike the Painted Lady's caterpillars, do not eat thistles, they eat nettles—you really have to admire the contribution the Red Admiral makes to our summer environment. I also like the way it chooses a sunlit patch of ground, and patrols it at high speed between basking periods on the ground or a tree trunk. This butterfly appears to be territorial, and it defends its favourite area vigorously against intruders, be they other admirals or not.

WINGSPAN: 50 mm.
HABITAT: widespread in forest clearings.

Up close, you can see that this butterfly has a thick body, powerful flight muscles and stout, angular wings, for rapid, super-controlled flight. When you find one in spring, it is usually quite worn and dull, with wing markings that are closer to pale orange than red. But when the summer generation emerges, the colours are dark and saturated, and the body is clothed in thick, brown hairs.

COMMON WOOD NYMPH

Cercyonis pegala

You've probably already seen this butterfly, but given it little thought. Just about any grassy field in July will have at least a few Common Wood Nymphs fluttering around and bobbing up and down at about the height of the tallest seed heads. Follow one, and you'll soon give up on getting a better look—they almost never sit still, and you rarely see them at a flower. Like all other butterflies, however, they have to sleep.

The sun comes up mighty early in July, and the birds come up with it, searching for food among the dew-covered meadows. Wood nymphs, like other butterflies, don't start flying until much later in the morning—sometimes not until 10 a.m. or so—which means they spend five or more hours sitting in the open, running the risk of being eaten. That's why they have a set of fake eyespots on their forewings that can be flashed at a predator if the need arises. Birds are not too bright, and they often fall for the bluff, thinking they have disturbed the slumber of some glassy-eyed reptile. It really is too bad that these butterflies are not more inclined to show off their wings, because the males have a lovely purplish iridescence.

> **WINGSPAN:** about 60 mm.
> **HABITAT:** grassy areas, mostly in the south.

MONARCH
Danaus plexippus

The Monarch is our most famous butterfly and one of our biggest as well. Most people know the facts: the Monarch is a migrant, and our local population returns each winter to a few small areas in northern and central California, where they spend winter alongside the rest of the Monarchs from the west coast of North America. Another exciting part of this story is that the Monarchs we see here are the grandchildren of the generation that overwintered in California the year before. No one quite knows how they find their traditional wintering grounds, having never been there, but they do. Sadly, all of their wintering areas are threatened by development.

WINGSPAN: about 95 mm.
HABITAT: fields and meadows in the southern Interior.

These butterflies make this great migration against huge odds, but they are partly protected by their body chemistry. As a caterpillar, each Monarch feeds on the leaves of milkweed plants, and chemicals in the leaves make both the caterpillar and the butterfly distasteful to birds. The distinctive orange and black colours on the Monarch advertise this fact, and another butterfly—the Viceroy—copies the colours to help protect itself. The Viceroy (*Liminitis archippus*) has not been seen in B.C. for many years now. Viceroys are smaller than Monarchs but where they occur together, the birds don't seem to notice.

POLYPHEMUS MOTH

Antheraea polyphemus

When a Polyphemus Moth comes flapping in to the porch light, everyone takes notice. This moth is one that many people assume is a butterfly, because it is so amazingly beautiful. The antennae tell the real story: moths have fuzzy antennae or thin and pointy antennae; butterflies have slender antennae with thickened tips. The antennae of the male moth are not feelers but smellers, and they pick up the faint aroma of the female's perfume. Following the scent upwind, the male finds his mate in the dark.

When daylight comes, Polyphemus Moths generally roost with their wings above their backs. If a bird tries to peck at them, they suddenly spread the wings to expose their fake eyes. Most birds are startled by this display, but the fake eyes don't fool all predators. If you find a pile of wings

> **WINGSPAN:** about 110 mm.
> **HABITAT:** southern forests.

on the ground, you'll know that this tactic didn't work. The name "Polyphemus" comes from a one-eyed giant in Greek mythology—too bad the moth has four fake eyes and two real ones, for a total of six. Polyphemus caterpillars, by the way, are bright green, are shaped like an extended accordion and feed on such things as birch and dogwood leaves.

CALIFORNIA SILK MOTH

Hyalophora euryalus

About the same size as a Polyphemus Moth (p. 43), this one is less common. As such, it generates even more excitement when it appears around people. Along with the Polyphemus, it is a member of the giant silkworm family, a separate group from the commercial silkworm of Asia. At one point, the possibility of using giant silkworms for making silk for sale was explored in North America. It turned out that they wrap too many leaves and messy knots into their cocoons, so the plan failed. Thus, the giant silkworms remain symbols of the wild.

WINGSPAN: about 100 mm.
HABITAT: shrubby areas throughout B.C.

In more populated regions, they are gradually decreasing in numbers as habitat is destroyed and moths spend their lives flapping around light bulbs, instead of mating and laying eggs. Adult giant silkworms are among the bugs that have no mouths and live off body reserves once they emerge from the pupae. If you find one, and it poops a light brown liquid, don't be alarmed. The liquid is "meconium" and consists of the wastes left over from the transformation from caterpillar to moth. This moth is often misidentified as the similar Cecropia Moth (*H. cecropia*) that only lives in eastern North America.

HERA BUCK MOTH
Hemileuca hera

T he buck moths are also members of the giant silkworm family (see pp. 43–44), despite the fact that they are not particularly gigantic. The wings are, however, very boldly patterned in black and white, and the furry bodies are usually patterned with bright red

WINGSPAN: about 60 mm.
HABITAT: open areas in the southern Interior.

and yellow tufts of hairs. Most often, people notice them as they rest on vegetation near ground level, often in the act of mating. They are day-flying moths, and their flight is fast and frantic. Mid-day is the time when they are most active. The caterpillars feed on various sorts of sagebrush leaves, and the hairs on their bodies can sting you if you touch them. The result is a temporary rash, and one should always remember that hairy caterpillars are not always safe to handle, no matter how cute they might appear. In other parts of the world, caterpillars can send you to the hospital.

As you go further south, the number of buck moth species increases to about 18, and they are the most diverse group within the giant silkworm moth family in North America. The American Southwest is the buck moth hot spot, and bugsters are still struggling to discover how many species there are, and how to classify them.

SHEEP MOTH
Hemileuca eglanterina

T he Sheep Moth is technically a type of buck moth (because it is a member of the genus *Hemileuca*), and like the others in this group, it flies by day. Older books place this species in a separate genus, *Pseudohazis*—it not being a typical-looking buck moth. It has broader wings, and a slimmer body, and this combination makes the Sheep Moth look a lot like a butterfly at first glance. Still, Sheep Moths have furry antennae—a sure sign that they are moths and not butterflies—and despite the fact that they are active during the day, they still rely heavily on chemical communication to find their mates (the antennae are used to smell for prospective mates).

WINGSPAN: 50–65 mm.
HABITAT: open areas in southern B.C.

Compared to the Nevada Buck Moth (*H. nevadensis*), this species has a much more intricate wing pattern, with "sunburst" edges and thick, graceful, black lines through the wings. Sheep Moths are also highly variable in colour: some individuals are almost pure black and white, while others are a deep orange colour overall. Colour variation is common in butterflies and moths, and it can serve a number of different functions, related mainly to courtship, camouflage or mimicry. Which is the case for the Sheep Moth, we still do not know. In late summer on warm afternoons, watch for Sheep Moths, flying high above the ground.

GREAT ASH SPHINX

Sphinx chersis

Sphinx moths are named for the way their caterpillars adopt a pose something like the famous Sphinx of ancient Egypt. Another name for this group is "hawk moths," based on their streamlined form and rapid flight. I prefer "sphinx," because the moths, unlike hawks, are not predators. In fact, they feed on flower nectar, and there are many sorts of flowers that open their petals and produce nectar at night, to accommodate these nocturnal pollinators. The proboscises of the sphinx moths can be extraordinarily long—sometimes longer than the moth's body and sometimes twice as long or more!

The Great Ash Sphinx is one of the largest moths in Canada, and it is a fairly typical member of the family. Despite its name, its caterpillars are not exclusively found on ash leaves. They will feed on a variety of tree species, including lilac, trembling aspen and cherry. The caterpillars are huge, of

WINGSPAN: about 110 mm.
HABITAT: shrubby and treed areas in the southern Interior.

course, and they never fail to attract attention as they march across roads and sidewalks on their way to a place to dig into the soil and form a pupa. The Great Ash Sphinx is never a common moth, and it is always interesting and exciting to see.

BIG POPLAR SPHINX

Pachysphinx modesta

A large female Big Poplar Sphinx probably has the heaviest body of any B.C. moth, and this species' caterpillar certainly qualifies as one of our biggest insects overall. The Big Poplar Sphinx is an uncommon find, and even experienced moth devotees are always thrilled when they see one. Most sphinx moths feed on flower nectar, but some, like the Big Poplar, are unable to feed as adults. They have no mouth, and in this way they are like the giant silkworm moths.

WINGSPAN: about 110 mm.
HABITAT: poplar forests in southern B.C.

Big Poplar Sphinxes also have fairly broad wings for a sphinx, patterned in subtle pastel hues, camouflaged on the front wing and smeared with blue and red on the hind wings. The outer border of the front wings has a wavy outline, which undoubtedly helps camouflage these moths during the day. Their eyes are difficult to see, hidden by the furry forehead and shoulders, and the combination of all these features probably gave this bug its scientific name, which is often translated as "Modest Sphinx." This name brings up an important point—bugs do not seem to possess a self-image, or anything we might recognize as an ego. At least, no one has ever produced any evidence to support the notion. Thus, without an ego, I doubt it is possible for any bug to be either modest, conceited or anything in between.

SNOWBERRY CLEARWING

Hemaris diffinis

Another name for this little creature is the "Hummingbird Moth." Sure enough, when one hovers in front of a flower, uncoils its long, beak-like proboscis, and shows off its handsome colours, you can't blame some people for thinking they are looking at a bird. In bird field guides, this clearwing is usually the only insect that warrants a picture. One friend of mine tells me that the first time she saw one, she crept up for a better look and then felt a deep sense of dread—she had no idea what sort of life-form she was looking at, and for a biologist that is a scary feeling.

WINGSPAN: about 40 mm.
HABITAT: open areas throughout B.C.

Of course, there is nothing to fear about these moths, and in fact they are quite delightful. They are members of the sphinx moth family, and they behave like most of their nocturnal cousins. The only things that set them apart from their relatives are the see-through wings and daytime habits. The caterpillars are typical of sphinxes and feed on a variety of forest plants. The adults are on the wing mainly in May. There are two, possibly three species of very similar clear-winged sphinxes in B.C., of which this one is the most common.

GARDEN TIGER MOTH

Arctia caja

Tiger moths are not especially big, but they include some of the prettiest moths of all. The Garden Tiger Moth is one of the largest in B.C. In a good year they are easy to find. Like many insects, their populations fluctuate greatly from year to year, easily able to bounce back from a bad year or two because the females lay huge numbers of eggs, and the most important thing determining the number of moths in a given year is the number of caterpillars that survive the early life history of the species.

WINGSPAN: about 55 mm.
HABITAT: forested areas throughout B.C.

The bright colours of tiger moths are there to warn predators not to eat them—they are filled with bad-tasting chemicals. Of course, their warning colours only work during the day. At night, when the main enemies of tiger moths are bats, they defend themselves in other ways. Some tiger moths can hear the bats coming, way above the range of human hearing. When they feel threatened, they make their own ultrasonic sounds, to warn the bat that it is about to get a mouthful of bad-tasting tiger moth. Tiger moth caterpillars are generally fuzzy, and the fuzz can cause itchiness and rashes. They even weave these hairs into their cocoons, so that the insect is protected at every stage of its life, both day and night.

CARPENTERWORM MOTH

Prionoxystus robiniae

T wo things set the Carpenterworm apart from most of the
other familiar moths of B.C. First, it

WINGSPAN: females about 70 mm
or more; males smaller.
HABITAT: southern forests.

shows "sexual dimorphism." Sexual dimorphism is the standard scientific
term for differences in the appearance of males and females. In the
Carpenterworm Moth, the male is small and has streamlined, pointed wings
like a sphinx moth (pp. 47–49). As well, the male's wings are more darkly
mottled and his hind wings are yellow. The female is larger, with broader
wings and a translucent grey pattern. Most likely, the male is adapted to find
the female from a distance, while the female is more of an egg-laying spe-
cialist. The second thing that sets this moth apart is that its caterpillars eat
wood, not leaves. The caterpillars dig tunnels in the wood of deciduous trees,
and, as you can imagine, they are large creatures. People often discover them
when splitting firewood.

Moth specialists often divide moths into the "macro-moths" and the
"micro-moths" and for the most part, the micros are indeed smaller than the
macros. The Carpenterworm, however, is the biggest of the micros, and a big
female can have a wingspan of 85 mm, dwarfing the vast majority of macro-
moths. Such is the power of tradition, where unsuitable names persist
despite their obvious flaws.

HORNET MOTH

Sesia apiformis

The Hornet Moth is a member of another very impressive group of "micro-moths," which are known as the clear-winged moths. Almost all of them look like wasps. The Hornet Moth itself is a mimic of the paper wasps, but other species of clear-winged moths mimic all manner of smaller stinging wasps. At a distance, it is not always easy to tell a Hornet Moth from a real wasp. Look for a slightly dumpier body, with a furry, rather than smooth, look to it—that's the moth.

I have not seen any studies on the subject, but it is possible that the mimicry goes both ways in this case. Whereas wasps have a painful sting, many members of the clear-winged moth family possess distasteful chemicals, and some are known to purposely extract these chemicals from plants by regurgitating onto bark and repeatedly sucking up their own digestive juices. So perhaps, as far as a bird is concerned, both Hornet Moths and hornets are to be avoided, and having only one colour pattern to remember helps the birds do so more easily.

WINGSPAN: about 35 mm.
HABITAT: shrubby areas in southern B.C.

Hornet Moth caterpillars, like Carpenterworm caterpillars (p. 51), feed inside wood and roots, mostly on poplars and willows. The moths are generally more common than one might think, because they go undetected so often.

CALIFORNIA TENT CATERPILLAR MOTH

Malacosoma californicum

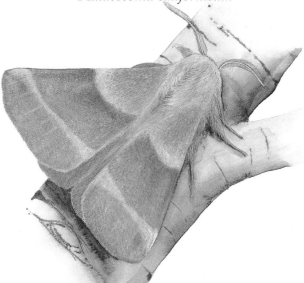

T his moth is probably best known as a caterpillar. The moth itself is not unattractive—furry and brown—but it takes an expert eye to recognize that it is a member of a relatively small family of furry, brown moths, the lappet moth family (Lasiocampidae). Most other brown, furry moths are either owlet moths (Family Noctuidae) or prominent moths (Family Notodontidae).

This species takes its name from the habits of its caterpillars. The female lays her eggs all together in an egg mass, and when the caterpillars hatch they stay together as well. They spin a silk shelter for themselves, in which they spend the daylight hours safe from birds and parasites. At night they venture out to feed on leaves, usually of poplars and willows. When they are ready to pupate, they wander away from the tent, and spin a cocoon about the size and shape of a perogie. The cocoons also contain a yellowish-white powder and are easy to recognize. Some years there are huge numbers of tent caterpillars, and they can be important pests, while other years they are rare. Parasitic flies and wasps, along with diseases, cause these tremendous fluctuations in numbers.

> **WINGSPAN:** about 35 mm.
> **HABITAT:** widespread in southern B.C.

BLACK WITCH
Ascalapha odorata

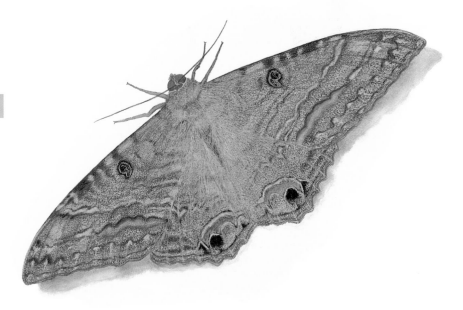

The Black Witch is our largest moth, but it's not really "ours," in a way. Every summer, a few of these impressive creatures turn up in B.C., flying to lights. Would you believe that each one of these moths was born somewhere in Central America? This tropical species disperses widely in all directions each and every year. On powerful elongated wings, these moths make their way north, becoming less and less common the further into Canada they go. It shouldn't surprise anyone to notice that the ones we find here are generally worn and faded, with torn wing edges and dull colours.

To fuel such a journey (longer than the flight of a B.C. Monarch, p. 42, to its wintering grounds in California), the moths feed each night, at sap or rotting fruit. Thus, they are drawn to the same sorts of bait that attract underwings, and in fact they are the largest members of the underwing subfamily of the owlet moths. Don't let their lack of a colourful hind wing fool you—they are still closely related. Males have longer, more pointed wings, while females have a light band through the middle of the wings.

WINGSPAN: up to 150 mm.
HABITAT: forested areas.

54

WHITE UNDERWING

Catocala relicta

The underwings are the moths of late summer. On occasion you see them by day, but for the most part they are creatures of the early evening, when they search for sap-flows and over-ripe fruit, on which to feed. Their coloration is remarkable, with camouflaged front wings and boldly coloured hind wings. At rest, the White Underwing blends perfectly with the bark of the paper birch tree, closing its front wings over the hind ones. If a bird discovers it, the moth spreads its wings and takes advantage of the brief startle effect to allow it a moment to escape.

> **WINGSPAN:** about 65 mm.
> **HABITAT:** forests in southern B.C.

If you want to see one of these moths, here's what to do: mix up a pot of beer, molasses, rum and lots of brown sugar. Warm the pot up to melt the sugar, then let it cool. Go outside and paint the mixture on the rough bark of poplar trees, then wait until after dark. Sneak up carefully with a flashlight, and try not to snap any twigs. The moths have good hearing, and they will sometimes flee at the slightest sound. Of course, after an hour or so of sipping the alcoholic bait, they seem less concerned about people, and more absorbed in their own inebriated thoughts.

AHOLIBAH UNDERWING
Catocala aholibah

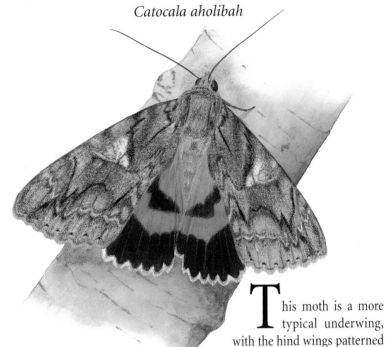

WINGSPAN: about 70 mm.
HABITAT: forests in southern-most B.C.

This moth is a more typical underwing, with the hind wings patterned in red and black. The pattern makes them easy to recognize as a group, but in B.C. there are a number of species that are so similar even the moth experts can't always agree on which is which. In some ways, this confusion only adds to the mystique that surrounds this group.

As well, many underwings have strange names that conjure images of bitter male entomologists who had difficulty with the women in their lives. Consider such species as the Mother Underwing, the Charming Underwing and the Forsaken Underwing. Then there are the Widow Underwing, the Girlfriend Underwing, the Sorrowful Underwing, the Betrothed Underwing, the Old Maid Underwing, the Consort Underwing, the Bride Underwing and the Old Wife Underwing. I guess the lesson here, to avoid the pain of love lost, is to spend more time with one's partner, and less out prowling in the dark. Unless, of course, you both like underwings, in which case you can enjoy looking for them together. Underwing caterpillars, by the way, are stream-lined and camouflaged, and most of them feed on poplars.

SPEAR-MARKED BLACK

Rheumaptera hastata

The wings of this familiar moth are patterned in black and white, with a delicately curvaceous outer margin. Its relatively light body struggles to flap the wings, and thus it doesn't whirr in flight like most moths—it flutters. In fact, there are only three sure signs that this one is not a butterfly. First, it has thin antennae with no clubs at the tips. Second, it flies by night. Third, it has a habit of crashing into leaves and branches when it flies, rather than deftly avoiding them.

The Spear-marked Black is a member of a large group of equally enchanting moths, the geometers. They are also called "inchworm moths," because their caterpillars perform the familiar inching-along motion when they travel. Their method of locomotion is also responsible for the names

WINGSPAN: about 35 mm.
HABITAT: forests in southern B.C.

"looper" and "spanworm." Many of the geometers are colourful, and some, like the Spear-marked Black, fly by day. Almost always, when someone comes to me with a "butterfly that isn't in the field guides," it turns out to be a geometer.

PACIFIC TIGER BEETLE

Cicindela oregona

Tiger beetles are exciting. They have long legs, they run fast, they have powerful jaws for killing other bugs and they have large eyes. Some, as an added bonus, are brightly coloured. The Pacific Tiger Beetle is widespread and common, but it is really one of the least colourful members of the group. These beetles live on moist sand and gravel, alongside both lakes and rivers. They generally like open ground with few plants, because they find it easy in such places to spot prey and run it down.

It's a shame more people don't get a chance to see tiger beetles. The reason for this unfortunate circumstance is simple—the beetles always see us first. They are quick to take wing, but they usually don't fly far. It's easy to watch where they land, and sneak up for a good look. If you watch tiger beetles, you'll see them chase down food, zip out after potential mates and attack any small piece of debris that might be an edible bug. They only come out on sunny days, mind you, so don't go looking for them in the rain—that's the time to stick to water beetles.

LENGTH: 12 mm.
HABITAT: widespread on riverbanks and beaches.

PRIMITIVE TIGER BEETLE

Omus spp.

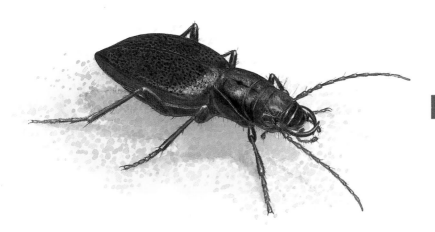

These beetles are also tiger beetles, but they are also a sort of missing link. With small eyes, nocturnal habits and a much slower running speed, Primitive Tiger Beetles act much like ground beetles, and not like typical tiger beetles. They are also coloured like a ground beetle, all black with no white markings or iridescence. These resemblances, plus others, have caused many specialists to declare that tiger beetles, in general, form a subgroup within the ground beetle family. However, Primitive Tiger Beetles also possess a type of jaws that are unique to tiger beetles, and their larvae are very typically tiger-beetlish as well. They live in vertical burrows in the ground, and ambush small bugs that walk by. No intermediate jaws or larvae are known, either living or fossil, to connect the tiger beetles and the ground beetles. Thus, it is also possible that the tiger beetles form an ancient lineage separate from the ground beetles. They are now a worldwide group, ranging in size and shape from big-eyed, tiny, tree-dwelling species to huge, long-jawed nocturnal tigers in South Africa. And the solution to the problem of classifying them may live right here in B.C., with the Primitive Tiger Beetles.

LENGTH: about 15 mm.
HABITAT: forest clearings in the southwest and on Vancouver Island.

SNAIL-KILLER CARABID

Scaphinotus angusticollis

Next time you are out camping in the moist coastal forests, spend a few extra minutes looking around with your flashlight when you make that inevitable trip to the biffy after dark. Over much of summer, you can expect to find a large, brownish-black ground beetle prowling the forest floor. It's called the Snail-killer Carabid, and it is an elegant beetle indeed. With an elongated head, a remarkably slender prothorax and a body shaped like a cartoon rowboat, the carabid is not your average ground beetle. Of course, there is no such thing as an average ground beetle, because in most places there are about as many species of ground beetles as there are kinds of birds. You wouldn't talk about an average bird, would you—half way between a hummingbird and a pelican? Snail-killer Carabids are adapted to eat snails and slugs, and their long heads help them get into those hard-to-reach places in snail shells and massive banana slug carcasses. They are specialized, unusual and a fascinating addition to the West Coast bug community. And with all those famous slugs to eat, it's no wonder they are abundant.

LENGTH: 20 mm.
HABITAT: moist coastal forests and on Vancouver Island.

FIERY HUNTER
Calosoma calidum

Here is another sort of a ground beetle, with its own fascinating story. Like the Snail-killer Carabid (p. 60), this beetle is one of the larger members of the family, but it differs from the Snail-killer in both its looks and its habits. The Fiery Hunter has hundreds of ruby red jewel spots set in its shining black wing covers. The spots really do look like jewels, even under a magnifying glass. And while the Snail-killer Carabid likes to rummage around among the dead leaves, the Fiery Hunter is also a fearless climber of trees. Day and night, it explores the woods for its favourite food—caterpillars. Even fuzzy tent caterpillars are to its liking. With

LENGTH: 20 mm.
HABITAT: forests in eastern B.C.

mighty jaws and a head as hard as a choke-cherry pit, the Fiery Hunter chews through the caterpillar's hairy defences and gobbles up the soft insides. This species is native, and one we can be proud of. Watch for the similar Frostbitten Hunter (*C. frigidum*), which looks a lot like the Fiery Hunter but is slimmer where the wing covers join the pronotum. As well, notice that you will sometimes find these beetles with green or golden, rather than red, jewel spots. These ones are not a different species, just a different variation on a lovely little theme.

BIG DINGY GROUND BEETLE

Harpalus pennsylvanicus

This ground beetle is by no means our biggest or most spectacular, but it's one that everyone should know. When you think that the average size of a beetle is about 2.5 mm, the Big Dingy takes its rightful place as one of the whoppers. Like most of its relatives, it is a predator—friend of the gardener and terror of insect life in the flower beds. In its appearance, this ground beetle is what biologists call "generalized." In other words, it doesn't possess any obvious body features that constitute adaptations for a specialized lifestyle (for example, the elongate head of a Snail-killer Carabid, see p. 60). This lack of obvious body features does not mean that the Big Dingy is a primitive ground beetle; it is more likely that the Fiery Hunter (p. 61) resembles the long-extinct ancestor of the group. Because there are so many ground beetles, there have also been many people who made it their entomological mission to study them. Luckily, I have been able to meet most of the living "carabidologists" myself. There is a rumour among these people that the so-called "dingy" ground beetles (technically the "harpalines") were given their common name by specialists in other sorts of ground beetles, as a playful dig at those who study the "dingy" ones.

LENGTH: 13 mm.
HABITAT: open areas in southern B.C.

BURYING BEETLE

Nicrophorus spp.

Somebody has to deal with them, and you know exactly what I am talking about. Yes, I'm referring to dead mice. Without nature's help, the world would be knee deep in them. That is where the beautiful, orange-and-black Burying Beetles fit into the grand scheme of things. Flying low over the ground, just before sundown, they spread their many-leaved antennae to the wind, and sniff. They seek the unmistakable aroma of today's death. If they find a big carcass, such as a deer or a coyote, they join their necrophagous buddies for a quick snack. On the other hand, if they find a dead mouse, or some other tiny corpse, they rejoice.

LENGTH: 15 mm.
HABITAT: a variety of habitats throughout B.C.

A Burying Beetle's dream is to find a dead mouse, and a husband or wife, all in the same evening. Then, they can bury the treasure, kill the maggots that might steal some of the meal, and push the cadaver into a ball. Next they lay their own eggs and start a family. The beetle grubs raise their little heads to beg for food, and in response Mom and Dad give them bits of putrescence to eat. Now isn't that nice? Who said that beetles don't possess the ability to show complex behaviour and tender parental care?

HAIRY ROVE BEETLE
Creophilus maxillosus

To most people, a rove beetle doesn't look much like a beetle at all. It is a long, slender insect, and its wing covers are short—but a beetle it is and a good one at that. Beneath those wing covers are full-sized wings, folded so intricately that you'd swear they couldn't fit. The Hairy Rove Beetle is another one of those bugs that is attracted to death. Any carcass will do, and these beetles are some of the first to arrive after decomposition has set in. The Hairy Rove Beetle is not there to eat the meat, mind you. Instead, it is there to ambush the unwary. A dead animal is a magnet for bugs, after all. So the Hairy Rove Beetle prowls the cadaver and dines on flies, maggots and various other beetles.

LENGTH: up to 20 mm.
HABITAT: open areas throughout B.C.

Rove beetles form a diverse family of beetles, but most are very small. There is another whopper in these parts, called the Pie-Killer (*Ontholestes cingulatus*). It prefers to do its fly hunting on top of cow "pies." When it feels threatened, it curls its long abdomen up over its back, and exposes yellow bands between the segments, making it look frighteningly like a Yellow Jacket wasp (p. 83).

MAY BEETLE

Phyllophaga spp.

T he first thing to know about May Beetles is that you don't always see them in May. May is, however, the best month to find them, and they are tough to ignore when you do. These are big, fat, clumsy, stupid beetles that fly around at night and are strongly attracted to lights. So, when you are sitting outside on that first warm evening in spring, you hear something like "bzzzzh… bzzzahssszzzzzzzzzzss…. PFUT! bzt. bzt! Bzzzzzt… bzzhssssss… bzt." That's the sound of a May beetle on a collision course with the porch light, after which it falls on its back and can't find its feet.

Kids like them, because you can find them in the morning (if hungry birds don't find them first), and they are fun to play with. They don't eat

LENGTH: 15–20 mm.
HABITAT: in forested areas throughout B.C.

once they become adult beetles, therefore they don't bite! May Beetle grubs grow up underground, where they feed on roots for three whole years. However, they are never common enough here to be real pests. May Beetles are members of the grand and glorious scarab beetle family, and they share with other scarabs such features as spiny legs, a sturdy body and many-leaved antennae.

65

TEN-LINED JUNE BEETLE
Polyphylla decemlineata

T his beetle is our largest scarab beetle. Its antennae are especially awesome, especially on the males. They look a bit like moose antlers, but being many-leaved, they give the impression of a bull moose with seven sets of antlers all stacked up on one another. When a male spreads this magnificent fan to the wind, the scent it seeks is that of the female. These beetles do not live long once they emerge, and they spend all of their time searching for mates and laying eggs. In general, the life history of this species is much like that of the May Beetle (p. 65), although the June Beetle quite naturally comes out mainly in July. The colour pattern of this beetle is also fascinating. If you look closely, with a magnifying glass, you'll see that the stripes on the wing covers are made up of tiny overlapping scales. The scales are pointed at one end, and rounded at the other, and some are white while others are tan. They are set in a background of amber-coloured cuticle, and each scale is as polished as a piece of hard wax. On the underside of the body, scales mix with long, beige hairs to give the beetle an almost cuddly look.

LENGTH: 25 mm.
HABITAT: widespread in southern B.C.

GOLDEN JEWEL BEETLE
Buprestis aurulenta

Among those who love beetles, another famous family is the metallic wood-borers. Scientists call these beetles "buprestids," and they are also known as "jewel beetles." Many of these insects are large, iridescent and almost robotic in their movements. They thrive in the heat of summer, and the best place to find them is on the sunlit sides of trees, where they meet their mates and lay the eggs that will become their "flathead borer" larvae.

One of the finest metallic wood-borers in B.C. is the Golden Jewel Beetle. It is widespread, because its larvae live inside a variety of coniferous trees. The adult beetle is a lovely iridescent green, with shining orange trim all around the wing covers. Once you learn where to look for them, you'll find jewel beetles in most places that have trees (and even some that don't). The colours of the Golden Jewel Beetle are unmatched by any other B.C. species, but this family of beetles is worldwide and in the tropics there are big, beautiful species that make ours look puny by comparison. In southeast Asia, many of the most colourful buprestids are often made into real jewellery, set in gold with their legs removed, and sold for a high price.

LENGTH: 17 mm.
HABITAT: forests in southernmost B.C.

PINK-FACED JEWEL BEETLE

Buprestis lyrata

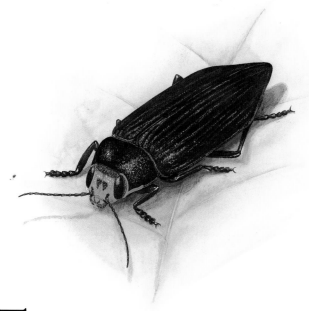

This jewel beetle is one of my favourite beetles in B.C., and I still remember the first time I saw one, on a family visit to the Gulf Islands. Jewel beetles are a distinctive group of beetles, but the easiest way to recognize them is to become familiar with the look in their eye. The way the eyes, mouthparts and antennae of jewel beetles come together gives them a characteristic look. The Pink-faced Jewel Beetle is one of the easiest of all to recognize, because it has bold pink markings (actually yellowish-orange when you look up close) on its face, as well as on the underside of the tip of its abdomen. It is not the most colourful jewel beetle, but it is still quite handsome. Its larvae are typical, flattened wood-boring grubs, with no legs and an expanded head and thorax. It lives in pine and fir trees.

LENGTH: 17 mm.
HABITAT: forests in southern B.C.

Like most other North Americans, I used to call this family of beetles the metallic wood-boring beetles. I adopted the more European name "jewel beetles" after spending time with a Swedish entomologist, who pronounced it "yuel beedlz" and considered them part of the broader category of "vood beedlz." Being part Swedish myself, I was an instant convert.

WESTERN EYED CLICK BEETLE
Alaus melanops

The Western Eyed Click Beetle is the largest member of the click beetle family in B.C. It is instantly recognizable not only by its size but also by the two eyespots on its pronotum. Because the beetle lives mostly in rotten wood and under bark, the eyes probably serve to startle predators who discover the beetles while searching in these places.

This family of beetles is very diverse, and most of its members are confusingly similar in a generally brown and featureless way. Still, they all share the amazing characteristic that gives the family its name—the "click." Turn one over on its back, and it will flail with its legs for a moment or two.

LENGTH: about 30 mm.
HABITAT: forests in the Interior.

Then, it arches its body, and suddenly PUNG!… it flips end over end into the air and, like a tossed coin, lands back on its feet roughly half the time. The truth is, however, they probably click for another reason. In nature, it is doubtful that they fall on their backs on a perfectly flat surface very often. Instead, the click probably functions to startle predators, and some types of click beetles can use the click to launch themselves into the air even before they are upside-down.

BEER BEETLE
Glischrochilus quadrisignatus

I realize that not everyone reading this book will be a beer drinker, but for those of you who are, you'll know this beetle for sure. Imagine yourself on the patio, tossing back a frosty mug of draft. Suddenly, swimming in the suds, you discover a handsome black beetle with a few yellow spots. It's a Beer Beetle! You fish it out with your finger and flick it away, and another one has taken the plunge before you know it. They get in people's hair, run around on the table and if you know something about them, they can be a great source of conversation. They certainly do no harm.

LENGTH: about 6 mm.
HABITAT: widespread, but some people seem to find them more easily than others.

Beer Beetles (some people call them "sap beetles," but we're not sure what *they've* been drinking) are naturally attracted to things like rotting fruit that lies fermenting on the ground. It may come as a surprise to some to discover that people did not invent alcohol. In fact, rotting fruit can become about as potent as a light beer. As far as a Beer Beetle is concerned, one is as good as the next, but generally they don't drown in rotting fruit.

SOUTHERN LADYBUG
Harmonia axyridis

Ladybugs eat aphids, and because aphids eat crops and garden plants, ladybugs are considered good. Back in the 1920s, entomologists figured that more kinds of ladybugs would mean more goodness, so they brought the Southern Ladybug over from Asia and released hundreds of them in Washington State, Delaware and Georgia. The Southern Ladybug is now the most common species on both the East and West coasts, and it is rapidly colonizing the centre of the continent as well. In some places, it has become notorious for its habit of invading buildings by the hundreds of thousands in preparation for winter hibernation. Somehow, no one anticipated this habit when the species was imported to North America.

To those of us who care about our native ladybugs, the Southern is now the bad guy. It's hard to be too angry with them, mind you. After all, they are still ladybugs, and among beetles the ladybugs are almost everyone's favourites. It's just too bad we think of them as little employees, sent out into the fields to do a job for us by killing our pests. Like us, they are just trying to make a living.

> **LENGTH:** 5 mm.
> **HABITAT:** so far, widespread in the Interior and the southern coast.

TWO-SPOT LADYBUG
Adalia bipunctata

"There are ladybugs in my house, and it's the middle of winter—what should I do?" Entomologists hear this quite often, and before the Southern Ladybug (p. 71) arrived the ladybugs usually turned out to be Two-spots. They get into your house in fall, looking for a comfy place to hibernate. Then, somewhere in January or February, some of them figure it must be spring, so they start looking for a way out. If you find these misguided beetles on your window panes, you can put them in a cooler place in the house and hope they go back to sleep, or you can offer them a small morsel of liver-flavoured cat food as a snack. Apparently, to them it tastes like aphids. Of course, if you have any aphids on your house plants, they prefer them to the cat food.

This ladybug is a lovely native species, and it is also amazingly variable. Most have two black spots on a red background, while others have four spots or two red shoulder patches on a black background. After a while, you can recognize them across the length of a room, just by their size and shape.

LENGTH: 4 mm.
HABITAT: trees, shrubs and buildings throughout B.C.

THIRTEEN-SPOT LADYBUG
Hippodamia tredecimpunctata

Like all beetles, a ladybug begins life as an egg and then hatchs into a larva. The larva of a ladybug looks something like a long-legged caterpillar, and it eats the same thing as the adult—aphids. Between the larval stage and the adult stage, there is a resting pupa stage, as with all beetles. The Thirteen-spot Ladybug is a native species, and it is common in grassy fields, lawns and gardens. Unlike many of its relatives, it is orange rather than red, and it is more elongate than most other ladybugs as well. When identifying ladybugs, look at the colour, the arrangement and number of spots, the pattern on the pronotum and the overall shape of the beetle. The thing that confuses some people is that a Thirteen-spot Ladybug is not just an older, bigger Two-spot Ladybug (p. 72). It is a separate sort of critter altogether; in fact, it is a separate species.

LENGTH: 6 mm.
HABITAT: open areas throughout B.C.

Once they emerge from the pupae, ladybugs don't change their spots, nor do they grow in size. They also don't change their spots to predict weather, as some people once believed. What a strange view of nature! As if one creature exists only to help another one survive—the ultimate in selflessness. Sorry, it just isn't true.

SPRUCE SAWYER
Monochamus scutellatus

Everyone who loves beetles dreams of the tropics. There, most of the beetles are much like our own, except that the biggest ones are much, much bigger. It is a thrill, then, to find a beetle in your own backyard that is a miniature replica of the great *Batocera* longhorn beetles of Asia and Australia. The Spruce Sawyer has an exotic look, with its white-flecked, ebony body, elegant shape and long, curved antennae. The male's antennae are longer than the female's, but the female is a bigger beetle overall. These marvellous creatures emerge in midsummer, from pupae that are formed just below the bark, inside dead spruce trees. The larvae excavate long, winding galleries through the wood, and somehow the long- "horned" adults chew their way out of the wood without harming their antennae or their slender legs. When they take flight to find a mate, they are noisy and awkward, flying with their legs splayed out to the sides, and their bodies held straight up and down. When one accidentally crashes into a car or a person, the western forests predictably ring with the cry: "What the HECK is THAT!?"

LENGTH: 20 mm, not including antennae.
HABITAT: forests throughout B.C.

CALIFORNIA PRIONUS
Prionus californicus

If you think the Spruce Sawyer (p. 74) is reminiscent of the great *Batocera* longhorns, then no one can blame you if you imagine that the California Prionus is our own version of the greatest longhorn of all, *Titanus giganteus*. *Titanus* can be 15 mm long, lives in South America and once merited its own article in *National Geographic*. I see nothing wrong with appreciating bugs for their resemblance to tropical relatives. After all, the only thing *Titanus* has that the California Prionus lacks is size, and the Prionus is not a small bug! They are both leathery brown, with big eyes, powerful jaws and a spiked pronotum—all features of their sub-family, the "prionines."

LENGTH: up to 50 mm.
HABITAT: forests in western B.C.

I first encountered this insect on my birthday, somewhere back in my teens. I was on a family vacation in Parksville, Vancouver Island, lying sick in bed feeling sorry for myself. Then, the biggest beetle I had ever seen flew up and landed on the window screen. I couldn't catch it, but the intensity of that encounter made me forget completely about the flu, and what I had assumed would be a lousy day, with no party and no cake. The appearance of that beetle made sure it was a birthday I would never forget.

BANDED LAUREL BORER
Rosalia funebris

The Banded Laurel Borer is a longhorn beetle, but it doesn't have so many famous tropical relatives (see pp. 74–75). The longhorn beetles are a very diverse family, and thus systematists have divided it into subfamilies, in which the genera are arranged. Hard-core bugsters learn to recognize the subfamilies of longhorns, along with the subfamilies of scarab beetles and ground beetles. So, the Spruce Sawyer is a lamiine ("LAM-ee-ine"), the Prionus is a prionine ("PRY-oh-nine") and the Banded Laurel Borer is a cerambycine ("serr-am-BISS-ine"). Many cerambycines have colourful wing covers, and the Laurel Borer is one of the nicest. Bugsters sometimes call the whole family "bissids," an abbreviation of the technical term cerambycid ("serr-am-BISS-id").

LENGTH: about 25 mm.
HABITAT: forests in western B.C.

The larvae of the Banded Laurel Borer are wood-borers in deciduous trees, and the adults are often found on or near the trees themselves. Many cerambycines feed at flowers, and this one will too, at times. Look especially on the big white flowerheads of cow parsnip and related plants. The antennae of male Laurel Borers are longer than their bodies, while those of the female are shorter. As usual among beetles, however, the female has a heavier body—she is the one who carries the eggs.

BLUE MILKWEED BEETLE
Chrysochus cobaltinus

This insect is another one of those beetles that is so darn pretty you really can't walk past it without a second glance. It looks like a great big, carefully polished, shining, bright blue ladybug. Its body is round and plump, and its legs end in what might well be described as paws. In other words, it's a cute beetle and a gorgeous one as well. It is a member of the leaf beetle family, and sure enough, it eats leaves. In particular, the Blue Milkweed Beetle eats the leaves of dogbane and milkweed. These plants produce toxic chemicals to discourage animals from eating them.

The beetle also has chemical defences, and it will ooze droplets of distasteful liquid when grasped. The beetle's first line of defence, however, is the same as most other leaf beetles—it tucks its legs in and drops to the ground. The Blue Milkweed Beetle is the western equivalent of the Dog-

LENGTH: 10 mm.
HABITAT: open areas in southern B.C.

bane Beetle (*C. auratus*), and like its eastern cousin, it actually prefers dogbane plants to milkweed. Perhaps if western entomologists had written bug books before their eastern colleagues, the western bugs would not be so commonly confused with the eastern ones.

WOOD ANT
Formica spp.

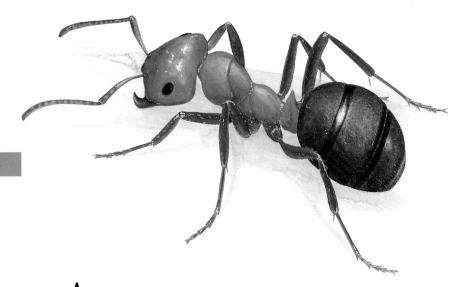

Ants are social creatures, and for this reason it is impossible to prevent some people from comparing them to us. In my opinion, to do so is a mistake. For one thing, ant societies are made up almost entirely of females that never reproduce. Imagine that in human terms, and hopefully you'll stop the comparison right there. If you need further convincing, picture a society where there is only one mother, and she gives birth dozens of times every day. I grew up believing that there are two kinds of ants—red and black—and that they are constantly at "war" with one another. Well, that's baloney, too. Some of the Wood Ants are actually "slave-makers." If you look closely at these ants, you'll see that they are both red *and* black. As well, the ant hills that this species lives in are sometimes home to black ants, running around among the red-and-black ones. These black ants were taken from their own nest when they were still pupae, and when they hatched they assumed they were among others of their own species. So they do work for the red-and-black ants, and neither sort of ant behaves as if anything unusual is going on. Now is that different from humanity, or am I just a mixed-up entomologist?

LENGTH: 4–8 mm.
HABITAT: forests throughout B.C.

CARPENTER ANT

Camponotus spp.

C arpenter Ants are not termites, and termites are not "white ants." They are both social insects, but ants have a pupal stage while termites do not. As well, all worker ants are adult females, while worker termites come in all ages and both sexes. Carpenter Ants are the biggest ants in the province, and they are also slow moving and not particularly aggressive. They have no sting, and, like the Wood Ants (p. 78), their main defence is to bite. Their jaws are strong, because they chew through wood for a living, and that is where they are similar to termites.

LENGTH: about 12 mm.
HABITAT: forests throughout B.C.

In the wild, you can spot a Carpenter Ant nest in a tree trunk by the pile of sawdust outside the entrance. They sometimes build their home inside the woodwork of houses and other wooden buildings, and there again the thing to watch for is sawdust. They don't actually eat the wood, but in the course of excavating their galleries, they certainly do weaken it, to the point where the tree, or the expensive house, may "fail," as the engineers say. Woodpeckers love to eat these ants, and it is fitting that our biggest ant is continually under attack from our biggest woodpecker, the Pileated Woodpecker.

BUMBLEBEE
Bombus spp.

Bumblebees have a painful sting, but they are so cute and fuzzy that we love them just the same. They are slow to anger, and quite docile, even when you are near their nest. In spring, queens set up new colonies in the abandoned burrows of mice and voles. There, they make wax pots, with open tops. Inside these pots they rear their grubs. Once the grubs grow up to be worker bees, the number of pots increases, and some are used to rear the young while others are filled with pollen or honey.

LENGTH: usually 10–20 mm.
HABITAT: clearings and meadows throughout B.C.

Bumblebees visit flowers to gather both pollen and nectar. Their wings are so small for the size of their bodies that some biologists were unsure for a while about how they could possibly fly. Because they are so hairy, bumblebee bodies look bigger than they are. The hair helps hold body heat when they fly, and they can fly at lower temperatures than many other bees. One friend of mine claims that when the bumblebees come out in spring, so do the bears, and when the bees go in for winter, the bears do, too.

BLUE HORNTAIL

Sirex cyaneus

Horntails are our largest sawflies, and sawflies are a group unto themselves, on par with bees, wasps and ants. In general, sawflies are pretty inconspicuous insects, but this one gets its share of attention. The adults are big, heavy-bodied and weird-looking, and the females have a pointed ovipositor that makes them look even more fearsome. Fortunately, they are not dangerous, and the ovipositor is not a sting. Instead, it is used to drill into the wood of trees, where the female lays her eggs, one at a time. The larvae are wood-borers, and some of the horntails are considered pests in some places. When the Blue Horntail gets into lumber, the tunnels of the larvae are conspicuous and difficult to hide.

LENGTH: 30 mm.
HABITAT: throughout B.C.

It is a general rule that the larvae of insects that go through a pupa stage are larger and heavier than the adults, because the transformation from one form to the other is accomplished without the intake of any food. Thus, horntail larvae are larger than horntails, just as caterpillars are larger-bodied than the butterflies and moths that they turn into.

BALD-FACED HORNET

Vespula maculata

If they didn't sting so much, these bugs would be some of our most watchable. They live in colonies, like honey bees, and they build huge paper nests, usually high in the branches of trees. To make the paper for the nests, they chew on bark, or wood, and mix the pulp with saliva. Then, they add each mouthful to the nest, forming either six-sided cells, where the larvae are reared, or the multi-layered outside cover of the nest. Because each load of pulp comes from a different source, you can see a subtle pattern of grey bands in the paper. If these hornets are coming to your fence or lawn furniture for pulp, you will soon notice a series of shallow grooves where they have chewed. For food, they visit flowers, catch bugs and are also attracted to fallen fruit and dead meat. By the time late summer rolls around, the nests are as big as basketballs, and the hornets are ready to defend them at the slightest provocation. In fall, the colony breaks down, and the nests don't last long, because birds pick them apart. Only the new queens survive winter, to start new colonies in spring.

LENGTH: about 13 mm.
HABITAT: forests throughout B.C.

YELLOW JACKET
Vespula spp.

Yellow Jackets are simply smaller versions of Bald-faced Hornets (p. 82), with yellow markings instead of white. It's too bad we can't just call them all by the same name—it does confuse people when the names "hornet," "wasp" and "jacket" are used interchangeably. It's a good example of a situation where the scientific names make more sense than the English ones (in scientific terms they are all species of *Vespula*).

Some Yellow Jackets nest in trees, like Bald-faced Hornets, while others make their paper nests in old rodent burrows in the ground (or in

LENGTH: about 10–15 mm.
HABITAT: widespread throughout B.C.

or under buildings). These nesting habits make them difficult to spot at a distance, and it is always a shock when you are walking through the bush and suddenly dozens of angry Yellow Jackets come swarming out of a hidden opening in the earth. You can't blame them—often the nests are discovered by Black Bears, who tolerate hundreds of stings while they dig up the nest and devour everything inside of it. Yellow Jackets, unlike honey bees, can sting repeatedly, although they do eventually run out of venom, I suppose.

PAPER WASP
Polistes fuscatus

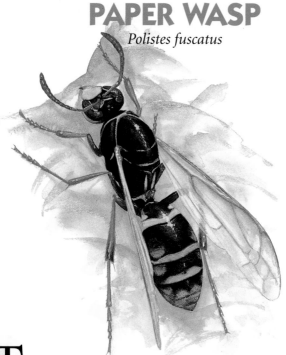

The name "Paper Wasp" really should go to Yellow Jackets (p. 83) and Bald-faced Hornets (p. 82). The "real" Paper Wasp is an amateur by comparison. Its nest is constructed beneath an overhang of some sort and has no outside covering. The single layer of paper cells is open to the air, and these wasps never build a second or a third layer. Still, it is interesting to watch Paper Wasps at the nest, because you can actually see what they are doing—something that can't be said of Yellow Jackets or Bald-faced Hornets. Paper Wasp colonies are of moderate size, to match the moderate size of their nests.

Paper Wasps feed at flowers, especially goldenrod, and they also hunt insects for food. Few people get stung by Paper Wasps, despite how common they are—our local species is not a particularly defensive one, which is lucky, because its sting is painful. To most people, the Paper Wasp is what a "wasp" should look like: long and slender, with a tiny "waist" and narrow wings. Most newcomers to entomology are surprised to discover that there are thousands of other insects called wasps, many of which are tiny and compact, and most of which are not even social.

LENGTH: about 18 mm.
HABITAT: open areas in southern B.C.

STUMP STABBER

Family Ichneumonidae, Subfamily Pimplinae

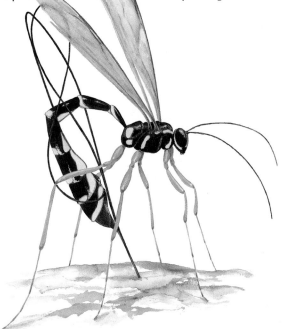

Talk to foresters about bugs and a few familiar species will come up time and again: metallic wood-boring beetles, long-horned beetles, horntails and ichneumons, also called Stump Stabbers. A big female ichneumon can be 85 mm long, including its immense ovipositor, and it looks like something that could definitely hurt you. In fact, many people think it does sting, despite the assurances of entomologists to the contrary.

If you find one, follow it. The Stump Stabber flies from tree trunk to tree trunk, all the while rapidly drumming its antennae while running around on the bark, quite obviously searching for something. Then, suddenly, she stops. Somehow, she has detected a wood-boring grub, deep in the wood.

LENGTH: with ovipositor, up to 85 mm.
HABITAT: forests throughout B.C.

At this point, she brings her ovipositor to bear, like some sort of strange miniature oil rig. The insect strains to work the tool into the wood, and eventually she finds the larva and forces a slender, very compressible egg down the tube and into the body of her host. There, the egg will hatch and the Stump Stabber grub will proceed to devour its victim from the inside out, eating the essential organs last.

85

THREAD-WAISTED WASP

Ammophila spp.

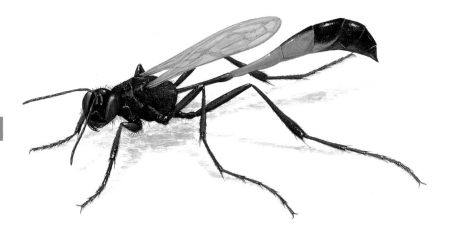

Most wasps are solitary, not colonial. The Thread-waisted Wasp is a member of the digger wasp family, and it has fascinating habits. The females sometimes take nectar from flowers, but for the most part they spend their days looking for caterpillars. With amazing agility, they sting the caterpillar in the nerve cord, and inject a paralyzing poison. The caterpillar is immobilized, although still alive.

With immense power and determination, the wasp then carries the caterpillar back to a burrow that she prepared some time before. She opens the burrow, drags the caterpillar down into the dark, and lays an egg on it. Next she comes back to the surface and closes the entrance, sometimes smoothing it over with a pebble held in her jaws. At this point, the wasp

LENGTH: up to 30 mm.
HABITAT: open bare areas throughout B.C.

goes off to look for another caterpillar or dig another burrow. Meanwhile, the egg hatches, and the wasp grub devours the body of the zombie caterpillar. That is, unless some other insect, such as a velvet ant or a parasitic fly, gets its egg into the burrow before it is closed. Then, the invader kills the baby wasp, and eats the caterpillar itself.

SPIDER WASP
Family Pompiliidae

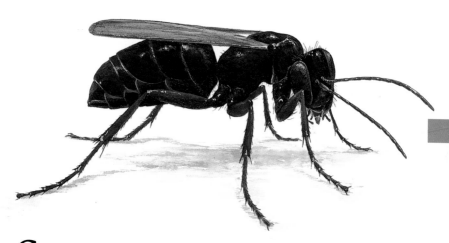

Spider Wasps resemble digger wasps in both form and habits, but they specialize in paralyzing spiders. In fact, they form a separate but related family within the overall category of "hunting wasps." Usually, they are at least partially black in colour, and many of them have shiny, iridescent blue-black wings.

The most famous member of the family is the giant Tarantula Hawk that lives in the deserts of the American Southwest. Naturalists have long been fascinated by the way these huge, fearless wasps search out tarantula spiders many times their own body weight, and then deftly avoid the spider's great, terrible fangs while maneuvering into position to deliver a paralyzing sting. After that, the Spider Wasp conducts itself much the same as most other hunting wasps do, complete with burrow in the ground and a single egg. For our B.C. species, the same dramatic story holds true, but the wasps are so small that no one notices them, and the spiders that fall prey to their macabre rituals are less imposing than a huge tarantula, at least to us. Still, if you get the chance to watch them, any of the hunting wasps can provide hours of good bug-watching entertainment.

LENGTH: 10 or more mm.
HABITAT: open bare areas throughout B.C.

87

HOVER FLY

Syrphus spp.

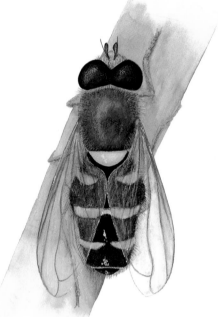

It is important to learn to recognize Hover Flies—it will improve the quality of your life. Why? Because, to protect themselves from harm, many Hover Flies look like wasps, but Hover Flies don't sting, and they don't bite either. Knowing a real wasp from a fake one would be helpful. Look for long antennae and a cylindrical abdomen—that's a wasp. If you see tiny antennae and a flattened abdomen—that's a Hover Fly (careful—some wave their front legs as if they were antennae!).

LENGTH: about 10 mm.
HABITAT: widespread throughout B.C.

In England, many people study Hover Flies as a hobby, and there they enjoy the luxury of being able to buy colour field guides to their local species. Perhaps some day we will reach the same level of sophistication here, but for the moment just recognizing Hover Flies at all is a good thing. It is also important to appreciate how many Hover Flies are involved in the pollination of flowers, because they visit blossoms the same way bees do. The larvae of Hover Flies are interesting, too. Some larvae are predators that feed on aphids, while others are the famous "rat-tailed maggots" that live in the muck at the bottom of shallow ponds.

HORSE FLY

Hybomitra spp.

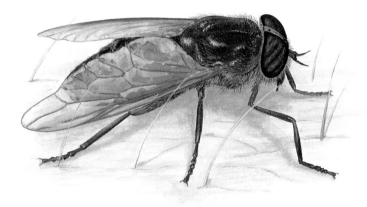

So what could be interesting about a Horse Fly? Well, how about the colours in its eyes? If you get a close-up look at one—perhaps after a lucky swat—check out the eyes and the intense rainbows that enliven its otherwise evil-looking face. These flies feed on blood, and they are most common near lakes. Go for a swim in a mountain lake (oddly enough, they are uncommon in the Okanagan), and I guarantee that by the time you have dried yourself off you will have taken at least one swing at a Horse Fly. They are attracted to large mammals (such as ourselves), and what also attracts them is a dark object with a light spot on it where the sun forms a reflective "highlight." If you drive a black car, or a black van, you will find even more of them when you get back to the parking lot.

LENGTH: about 15 mm.
HABITAT: open areas near water, throughout B.C.

One good thing about Horse Flies is that they are so big it's hard for one to bite without you knowing it is there. As well, Horse Flies have large blades in their mouthparts, rather than sophisticated slender stylets like a mosquito. A smaller version of a Horse Fly, with dark markings on its wings, is called a Deer Fly (*Chrysops* spp.). Given the chance, mind you, Horse Flies will bite deer, Deer Flies will bite horses, and either one will bite people, any chance they get.

BEEISH ROBBER FLY

Laphria spp.

Robber flies don't really steal things, other than life itself. They are amazingly agile predators, and they kill by catching other insects in mid-air. Between hunts, they find a perch on the ground or on vegetation, and from there they scan for potential victims. With large compound eyes, they have excellent vision and an amazing ability not only to spot their prey, but also to follow it through the air in high-speed pursuit. When they catch something, they return to the ground, with their fearsome proboscis deep in the tissues of their unlucky prey. They are not too distantly related to Horse Flies (p. 89), and they have a similar look overall.

LENGTH: about 20 mm.
HABITAT: throughout B.C.

Even beetles can fall prey to robber flies, and the flies have perfected the perfect way to kill these heavily armoured insects. While the beetle is flying, its wing covers are spread, exposing the soft abdomen underneath. The robber fly sinks its mouthparts into the beetle's soft spot while the two are still in the air. Most robber flies are not mimics, but the Beeish Robber Fly looks so much like a Bumblebee (p. 80) that it is tough to tell the two apart without a close look.

GIANT CRANE FLY
Tipula spp.

"**A**aaaaaggh! A monster mosquito!" That's what most people say the first time they see a Giant Crane Fly, an event that usually occurs while the fly is resting on the foundation of a suburban house. There are many species of crane flies, but the giant ones are large and orange in colour and have a pointy tip to the female's abdomen. They look evil, but the truth is you couldn't ask for a nicer bug. These flies don't bite at all—they are actually sort of attractive—and even the larvae are unobtrusive, living as scavengers in the soil.

Some people also mistakenly call these flies "daddy long-legs," a term that is most often used in B.C. to refer to Harvestmen (p.143), which are a sort of arachnid. In general then, we are surrounded by confusion with respect to Giant Crane Flies, and hopefully this book will lead the way to dispelling our ignorance. Another frequent twist to the finding-one-in-your-garden story is the fact that they are often discovered while mating, end to end. When a mating pair is disturbed, the sight of two sets of wispy flailing wings, 12 immense dangling legs and two giant "mosquitoes" tugging in opposite directions makes for a spectacle that is, let's just say, "creepy" to all but the most devoted bugsters among us.

LENGTH: up to 25 mm.
HABITAT: forested areas throughout B.C.

SAND DUNE BEE FLY

Poecilanthrax willistoni

B ee flies look like delta-winged fighter planes, but they are neither fighters nor beeish by nature. You can generally recognize members of this family by their swept-back, dark-coloured wings, and the Sand Dune Bee Fly has a distinctive pattern that separates it from the others. Many species have clear wings, and some of these are easy to confuse with Hover Flies (p. 88).

LENGTH: about 12 mm.
HABITAT: throughout B.C.

The Sand Dune Bee Fly, true to its name, is found mainly on bare sand, in the company of both tiger beetles (pp. 58–59) and digger wasps (p. 86). This association is not a coincidence. The larvae of bee flies are parasitic maggots. Some are parasites of tiger beetle larvae, while others eat the paralyzed insects inside wasp burrows or the larvae of digger bees and wasps themselves. For many, including the Sand Dune Bee Fly, we really don't know what their "hosts" are, because no one has ever studied the matter. This lack of interest is odd when you think of how easy it is to watch these flies, but even if you saw them flying above a tiger beetle or a wasp burrow, flicking eggs into the opening, you couldn't say for sure that this action was their intention. After all, they will also flick eggs into the lace holes of your shoes.

SNOW CRANEFLY

Chionea nivalis

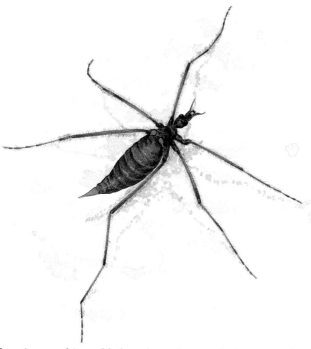

There is something odd about bugs that you find on snow. Snow Fleas (p. 122) are the most common, followed by all sorts of bugs that wind up on the snow by accident when they become active on a warm winter's day. The Snow Cranefly, however, is perfectly at home on the "white stuff," although it does require warm days to be active. It uses its long legs to stiffly transport itself across the frozen expanses, and it walks so slowly that you can clearly see how an insect uses its six legs. First, one set of three is put forward, like a tripod, followed by the other set of three. Long legs also hold the body at the correct height—too high and the air would chill the fly, too low and the snow would do the same.

LENGTH: about 3 mm; leg span about 10 mm.
HABITAT: widespread on open sandy ground.

These craneflies don't need wings, so they don't have any. In winter, wings only get a bug in trouble. As well, Snow Craneflies are dark in colour to help them warm up in the sun. All of these things make the Snow Cranefly one amazingly well-adapted animal. Don't confuse these flies with the Snow Scorpionfly (p. 96), which has a long head and a downward-pointed beak.

93

GREEN LACEWING

Chrysopa spp.

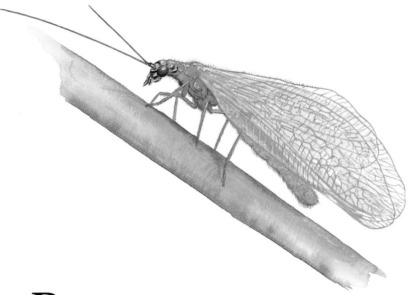

Beautiful, smelly and mean—that's how I think of lacewings. Green Lacewings are familiar garden bugs, and the adults are truly elegant with their many-veined wings, their delicate lime green bodies and their bulging golden eyes. The scientific name *Chrysopa* means exactly that: "golden eyes." Catch one, however, and you will soon notice a truly weird smell as it twists and turns in your fingers, while you hold it by the wings. The smell is a bit like coffee but not really.

As for the mean-spirited aspect of their nature, lacewings are predators, and they mostly eat aphids. Thus, they join ladybugs (pp. 71–73) and the larvae of some Hover Flies (p. 88) in a "friends of the gardener" category, despite the fact that none of them even know what a gardener is. Young lacewings, which are larvae much like those of a ladybug, are also aphid eaters. They are so vicious that the mother lacewing lays each egg on the top of a long, slender stalk, so the first larva to hatch doesn't eat all of its brothers and sisters before they can get out of the egg. Also, watch for Brown Lacewings, and even blotchy ones (both in the Family Hemerobiidae), usually early and late in the season.

LENGTH: about 10 mm.
HABITAT: forested areas throughout B.C.

94

SNAKEFLY
Agulla spp.

L ike the lacewings, Snakeflies are members of the insect Order Neuroptera. Some scientists place them in their own order, but they are clearly related to the other Neuroptera, as are beetles, oddly enough. The clues we need to unravel these relationships are now, unfortunately, more than 300 million years old, so you'll have to forgive entomologists for their confusion on this matter.

Snakeflies have an elongated head and thorax, and their front end looks a bit like a snake's head, so long as you ignore the six legs and lacy wings that lie behind. Snakeflies are predators on other small bugs, and they are often seen on flowers, or on vegetation. These are truly western bugs,

LENGTH: about 12 mm.
HABITAT: open areas in south-western B.C.

and in North America none are found east of the Rockies. As well, Snakeflies, in general, are a group that is found mainly in the north-temperate parts of the globe, and this group is almost completely absent from the tropics. As a West Coast bugster, I hope you take some pride in this nifty creature, which is often completely unfamiliar to your colleagues elsewhere.

SNOW SCORPIONFLY

Boreus spp.

Here's another bug that doesn't mind walking around on the snow. It is about the same size as a Snow Cranefly (p. 93), and it too is dark in colour to allow rapid warming by the weak rays of late winter sun. The elongate head of the scorpionfly easily distinguishes it from the cranefly, and the scorpionfly is also able to jump, which the cranefly never does. Snow Scorpionflies feed on mosses, a rare food plant among insects in general.

Scorpionflies form a distinct order of insects, and they are most closely related to two-winged flies and fleas. They go through complete metamorphosis, with a pupal stage. The scorpionfly gets its name from more typical members of the group, which have wings and an elongate, clasper-tipped abdomen that is carried over the back the way a scorpion carries its sting. Unfortunately, none of these wonderful bugs is found in our area. As a group, the scorpionflies are one of the most poorly studied of the insect orders. There appear to be about 500 species worldwide, and like most sorts of bugs they are most diverse in the tropics.

LENGTH: about 3 mm.
HABITAT: forested areas in southern B.C.

LACE BUG

Corythucha spp.

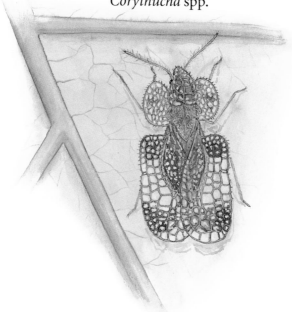

L ace Bugs are one of those things that you don't notice until you become a true bugster. Because they are small, they generally escape detection, but once you see one under adequate magnification, you'll be amazed at how intricate and elegant they are. You will come to realize, after a while, that given the proper equipment, it doesn't really matter how big a bug is—they are all equally intriguing when you get a good look at

LENGTH: about 3–4 mm.
HABITAT: forests throughout B.C.

them. My own first encounter with Lace Bugs came at about age six, and even then I was eager to accept the intrinsic coolness of a bug that is not among the biggies.

Lace Bugs are members of the sucking bug order, and they use their sucking mouthparts to suck the juices of plants. Some are pests, and the easiest place to find them is on the undersides of leaves. In winter, the adults often hibernate under loose bark. Lace Bugs get their name from their expanded pronotum, head and front wings, which are reinforced by an irregular honeycomb of struts and veins that gives a lacy appearance. These flanges are probably used to protect the bugs' legs from the attacks of tiny predators.

WESTERN BOXELDER BUG

Boisea rubrolineatus

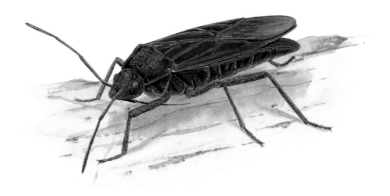

In many parts of Canada, this insect is referred to as the "Maple Bug," and people who have never heard it referred to by its official common name often "correct" my identification of this species and its relatives. It is true that these bugs feed mainly on the seeds of maple trees. In fact, the name "Boxelder" comes from an alternate common name for the Manitoba maple tree, *Acer negundo*, also called the ash-leaf maple.

Most people don't like Western Boxelder Bugs, because they have a habit of congregating in houses to spend winter. After all, when the family is gathering around the table for New Year's dinner, and a big clumsy Boxelder Bug goes buzzing across the room, bangs into the chandelier and lands in the mashed potatoes, who can blame anyone for taking offense? It is important, at moments like this, to remember that they don't do any harm, and that up close they are actually quite handsome. Bugsters will immediately recognize the function of their black and red colours—to warn predators that they taste bad (even though they don't smell bad). When they are young, they are even more colourful, more red than black. It is only when they get their wings, as adults, that the mainly black wings cover the bright red abdomen.

> **LENGTH:** about 12 mm.
> **HABITAT:** widespread in southern B.C.

ROUGH PLANT BUG

Brochymena spp.

S tink bugs stink. They do so with scent glands that produce a chemical with an odour unlike anything else that you or I are likely to ever encounter. This smell makes them easy to recognize up close, but they are also obvious in other ways. Stink bugs have broad, pointed shoulders and a large, triangular plate in the middle of their back (the scutellum, for those who like to know these things). Some stink bugs are more triangular than others, so if in doubt, sniff. Some feed on other insects, especially caterpillars, while others suck the juices from plants, or plant seeds.

Stink bugs are also known for their prowess as devoted mothers.

LENGTH: 13 mm.
HABITAT: widespread in southern B.C.

They lay a cluster of intricately sculptured eggs, all together on the surface of a leaf. Then the mother guards the brood until they hatch, at which point the babies are free to fend for themselves. Baby stink bugs, like all sucking bugs, are much like tiny adults but without wings. The Rough Plant Bug is one of our most abundant stink bugs, and it is a shame that it is not particularly colourful to bring it more attention. It is often found under the bark of dead trees in winter.

AMBUSH BUG
Phymata erosa

S mall but dangerous, that's an Ambush Bug. It isn't dangerous to people, mind you, but to any sort of insect that visits flowers, it is trouble. In the same fashion as a Goldenrod Crab Spider (p. 152), it lies in wait for the unwary pollinators, sometimes tucking in deep among the flower parts to hide. Our Ambush Bug is a yellowish colour, with large, angular flanges on the sides of its abdomen. Perhaps these flanges help break up its outline, and enhance its abilities as an ambusher.

Ambush Bugs have strong middle and hind legs that they use to hold tight to the flowers. Their front legs, on the other hand, are enormously strong for their size. These front legs are the "clutches" of the Ambush Bug, and with them it can subdue even a gigantic Bumblebee (p. 80) or a butterfly many times the size of the bug itself. Then, in typical predatory bug fashion, it injects a digestive fluid into its prey, waits for the insides of the insect to soften and then sucks the insides from its victims. I have seen these insects mainly in the latter part of summer, when they are easiest to find among the flowers of goldenrod plants.

LENGTH: about 9 mm.
HABITAT: open areas in southern B.C.

WESTERN OKANAGAN CICADA

Okanagana occidentalis

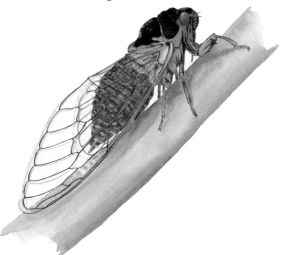

I n some parts of North America, cicadas are a big deal, especially when they emerge by the millions, cover the trunks of trees and drown out all other sounds with their incredibly loud buzzing. The larvae of these big insects live for years underground feeding on roots, and they emerge in early summer. Here in B.C., however, most people don't even know cicadas exist. To find one, you first have to learn what they sound like—a prolonged dry, rattling buzz. That's the male, and he sits on a slender tree branch while singing, often 3 m or more above the ground. If you are very stealthy, you may be able to get close enough to spot him. But make one false move, and he will either fly away or go silent on you.

LENGTH: about 22 mm.
HABITAT: forests in southern B.C.

The sound is produced by a vibrating mechanism in the abdomen, a resonating chamber and a thin membrane something like a banjo skin. Despite the size of cicadas, they can be incredibly noisy. Looking for cicadas will also introduce you to the Clay-coloured Sparrow, at least in some parts of the Interior. When I was young, I called these sparrows "Cicada Birds" because they sound so much like a cicada, down low in the grass—the first sign that something is amiss. And yes, the scientific name of this bug is indeed derived from the word "Okanagan."

NORTHERN ROCK CRAWLER

Grylloblatta campodeiformis

To find this amazing wingless insect, one has to venture high into the mountains and search among the rocky talus slopes and subalpine forests, or descend into the moist coastal forests and search among the soft mossy undergrowth. In the story of the Northern Rock Crawler, Canada holds a special place, because it was here that it was first discovered. In 1914 Edmund Walker, a Canadian entomologist, described the first Rock Crawlers from Banff National Park, of all places. He realized that he was looking at not only a new species but also a new genus, a new family and a new order—in other words, a whole new kind of a bug!

LENGTH: up to 30 mm.
HABITAT: cool mountainous areas in southwestern B.C.

Rock Crawlers, to entomologists, are interesting because they are so "primitive looking." That means they look like an "average" bug, from which a lot of others could have evolved. They have other interesting attributes to ordinary folks. For example, if you pick one up and hold it in your hand, the heat from your hulking mammalian body will kill it. That's how well adapted they are to cool climates. An adult Rock Crawler is likely to be seven years old, by the way, and they feed mainly on other insects, especially wingless craneflies.

FIELD CRICKET
Gryllus spp.

There is no more classic sound of summer than the chirping of crickets. Seeing one chirp, on the other hand, is no easy matter. If you do manage to get a peek, you'll find that it is only the males that make sounds. Males have two pointy things out the back of the abdomen (the cerci), while females have three (two cerci and one egg-laying ovipositor). To make the sound, male crickets rub their two wing covers (the thickened front wings) together, bringing a rasp into contact with a file. The hardened wing covers amplify and resonate to produce the noise we all know and love.

Field Crickets look a lot like House Crickets (*Acheta domesticus*), but House Crickets are brown while Field Crickets are black. The House Cricket, an introduced species from Europe, is the common cricket that you buy at pet stores to feed to pet frogs and lizards. The behaviour of House Crickets is much like that of Field Crickets, and they sound alike, too. So if you find yourself in bug-withdrawal somewhere around mid-winter, you can always stop by the pet store, buy a bag of crickets and go home with the chirping sound of a warm mid-summer's night. In B.C., the House Cricket cannot survive winter out of doors.

LENGTH: about 20 mm.
HABITAT: open areas in southern B.C.

CAVE CRICKET
Ceuthophilus spp.

C ave Crickets, in some places, actually live in caves. Here in B.C., however, they mostly live in rodent burrows, under rocks and logs and in rotten wood. What they want is a place that is moist and dark. For those who think *Homo sapiens* has advanced beyond the "caveman" stage, all I can say is—look in your basement. There, on occasion, you will indeed find a Cave Cricket or two. They need access to water and are therefore usually found somewhere near the floor drain. Don't let them worry you, because they do no harm. Some people mistake them for cockroaches, but I'm assuming that if you are reading this book, you'll do better than that.

Another name for Cave Crickets is "Camel Crickets," based on their hump-backed shape. Note as well that Cave Crickets have no wings, and therefore cannot chirp like other crickets. Ours have very long antennae, but the true cave dwellers have even longer feelers, as well as elongate legs. There is a painting of a Cave Cricket among the famous cave paintings of France, some 16,000 years old. It is the oldest depiction of an insect that has ever been discovered. As they say, "*plus ca change, plus c'est la même chose*"— "the more things change, the more they stay the same!"

LENGTH: about 12 mm.
HABITAT: widespread throughout B.C.

PRIMITIVE MONSTER CRICKET

Cyphoderris monstrosa

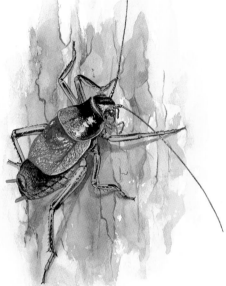

Whenever I go camping, in relatively dry pine forests near the end of summer, I look for this amazing bug. The males produce a characteristic trilling sound, and they are easy to find with a flashlight after dark, if you are stealthy and patient. Most of the time, they sit on the side of tree trunks, not more than 1 or 2 m above the ground. When you find one, I predict that you will be amazed by its black, white and pink coloration and the ferocious look in its eye.

Some entomologists consider this creature to be a "living fossil." What this expression means is that a once-diverse group of animals, well known in the fossil record, is now represented by only a few living survivors. In a way, I suppose all animals are "living fossils," but let's not get too philosophical about that here. Another interesting aspect of the behaviour of the Primitive Monster Cricket has to do with courtship. The male's hind

LENGTH: about 25 mm.
HABITAT: conifer forests in southern B.C.

wings are replaced by fleshy pads, and he raises his wing covers to allow the female to eat the pads right off his back—a nutritious gift that will probably help her develop healthy eggs as well.

RED-WINGED CLICKHOPPER

Arphia conspersa

This butterfly-like, band-winged grasshopper doesn't actually resemble any particular butterfly when it flies. On the hind wings, it is bright red with a black border. Many other species of band- winged grasshoppers are yellow with a black border, and these ones are supposed to look like sulphur butterflies. Perhaps the Red-winged Clickhopper resembles some sort of red-and-black butterfly that is now extinct, or perhaps to a bird the difference between red-and-black and yellow-and-black is not such a big deal.

When I am out on spring butterfly walks, there are plenty of false-alarm moments when people mistake a click-hopper for a butterfly that "landed here, in the grass someplace." Speaking of springtime, farmers and gardeners are used to thinking of grasshoppers spending winter as eggs and becoming numerous only in the latter part of summer. The Red-winged Clickhopper, in contrast, spends winter almost but not quite fully grown, and it moults to become an adult early in spring.

LENGTH: about 25 mm.
HABITAT: open areas in eastern B.C.

106

EUROPEAN EARWIG
Forficula auricularia

LENGTH: about 12 mm.
HABITAT: gardens and open areas in southern B.C.

Very few insects generate the confusion that earwigs do. For reasons that have never been clear, people often believe that they drill into human ears, that they are filthy and that they can pinch very hard with their cerci. According to entomologists, who should know, they don't do any of these things. As for how they got their name, your guess is as good as mine. The European Earwig is an introduced species, originally native to Europe, which arrived in B.C. around 1919. Thus, the name "earwig" is not of Canadian origin.

The reality of the situation is that earwigs are interesting, mostly harmless creatures, and that they are also good parents, who guard their eggs and newborn young. Some are parasitic on other sorts of bugs, while others are omnivores, predators, scavengers or plant feeders. It is the plant-feeding ones that we see most often, including the European Earwig. They especially like to feed on flowers, which naturally angers the gardener who grew the blooms. To my way of thinking, however, flowers grow themselves, and a flower with an earwig in it is infinitely more interesting than one without.

MINOR GROUND MANTID
Litaneutria minor

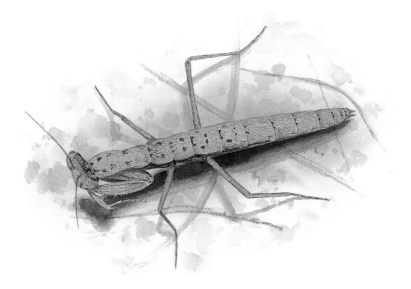

Praying mantids (or mantises, if you prefer) are well-known insects but uncommon in B.C. You sometimes see Chinese Mantids (*Tenodera aridifolia*) offered for sale in garden shops for control of pests in gardens, but this species is introduced (not native to this area). Chinese Mantids also could care less about pest control, but don't hold that against them. Another introduced species, the European Mantid (*Mantis religiosa*) is found with some regularity in the southern parts of the province.

Our one and only species of native mantid is the Minor Ground Mantid, and it is certainly an interesting one. Minor Ground Mantids live on the ground, or in low vegetation, and the females are wingless while the males have wings. They are grey-brown in colour, and they are active during both day and night. Like all other mantids, they can turn their heads to look in any direction they please, and they are lightning-fast predators, catching other bugs in their spiked forelegs. And yes, on occasion, a female will eat her mate during the act of copulation, and he will, indeed, continue mating, even without his brain. Apart from this last unfortunate feature, mantids are surely the most human-like of all bugs.

LENGTH: about 30 mm.
HABITAT: dry, open areas in the southernmost Okanagan.

GIANT STONEFLY

Pteronarcys californica

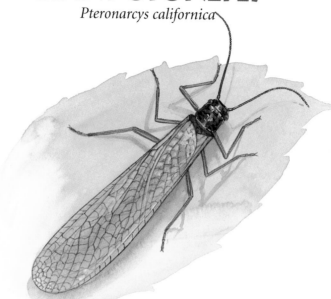

Adult Giant Stoneflies are encountered frequently by people walking near rivers—when they least expect it there is suddenly a huge, flattened insect crawling on their clothes, in a frenzied and highly unnerving manner. Of course, like most bugs, they can't harm you, and they don't want to harm you. Still, most people are introduced to stoneflies in this unsettling way.

Another way that many people get to know this group is by reading dinosaur books. When you look at the paintings of the amphibians and reptiles that "ruled the earth" before the

LENGTH: 40 mm, including the folded wings.
HABITAT: common along rivers and streams in B.C.

dinosaurs, there are often stoneflies added by the artist, along with other ancient sorts of bugs such as dragonflies and cockroaches. Leaving aside the fact that we all know that bugs, not dinosaurs, have *always* ruled the earth, it is interesting that stoneflies, as a group, have remained more-or-less unchanged for about 300 million years. They are also interesting to watch in the here and now, especially when they drum their abdomens on the stems of plants, as a courtship signal to the opposite sex. In flight, however, they are a far cry from masters of the air, proving that for almost a third of a billion years, it really didn't matter.

PACIFIC DAMPWOOD TERMITE
Zootermopsis angusticollis

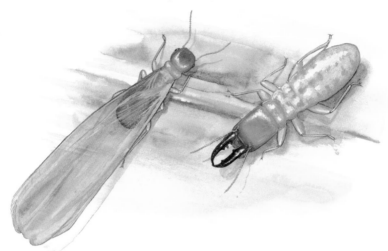

How lucky can you get? One of the biggest termites on earth lives right here in southwestern B.C. The workers are about 1 cm long, but a big soldier can be 2.5 cm long, with strong jaws—a very impressive bug. Unless you dig into rotting logs, the termites you are most likely to encounter are the winged ones, which are out on late summer flights to find a mate and then to attempt to start a new colony.

Termites are social insects, but they do not go through a pupal stage, so young termites look much like the adults and serve as workers for the colony. The colony is made up of both males and females, unlike ants, bees and wasps, in which all the workers are female. When they mature, termites can be workers, soldiers or winged "reproductives." Once the queen settles into the job of egg laying, she becomes bloated and helpless and is cared for by workers for her 20 or more years of life.

LENGTH: soldiers up to 25 mm.
HABITAT: southern coastal forests.

Termites eat wood, as anyone who lives in a wooden house knows, but they can't do it without some help. Approximately one third of their body weight is made up of microscopic protozoans. These "gut symbionts" digest the cellulose in the wood.

GERMAN COCKROACH
Blatta germanica

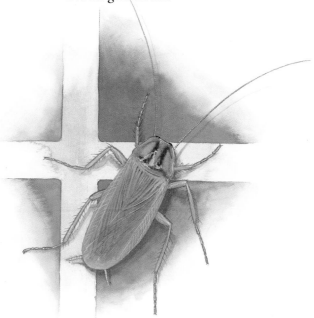

It is unfortunate for the German people that this cockroach is named in their country's honour. It is also unfortunate for the many thousands of harmless woodland cockroaches, living in the tropics around the world, that we temperate folks get such a poor introduction to their diversity and splendour. Of course, the cockroaches we find in this part of the world are all introduced, and they are all capable of "infesting" houses and other buildings.

German Cockroaches seem to especially like greenhouses. Once under a safe roof, they feed on just about anything edible, although they do need water, which they get from condensation or from water traps and drain-pipes. They are active after dark and very difficult to catch. Their cerci (the two feelers on the end of the abdomen) can detect even the slightest breezes, and cockroaches instantly run when they feel the pressure wave of an approaching foot. Cockroaches are very rarely implicated in the spread of disease, despite what you might hear. Generally, they are most abundant in places where things are most messy, and in those sorts of environments diseases have no problem getting around by themselves.

> **LENGTH:** about 15 mm.
> **HABITAT:** buildings; potentially anywhere in B.C.

BOREAL BLUET

Enallagma boreale

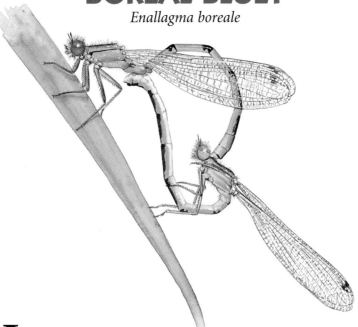

I f you have ever spent time beside a pond or a lake in May or June, you have seen these bluer-than-blue bugs. Like phosphorescent tooth picks, they hover among the reeds, where they catch their prey by plucking it off leaves while in flight. Aphids and baby grasshoppers are about the right size for a damselfly to tackle, and yes, Boreal Bluets are a type of damselfly. More specifically, they are a type of American bluet.

The males are patterned in blue and black, while some females are green or yellow, instead of blue. To be honest, our seven species of American bluets (in the genus *Enallagma*) all look more-or-less exactly alike. In cases like this one, entomology books usually say something like "identification is best left to specialists." In reality, it's not that hard—all you need is a good magnifying glass and some obscure information. More and more, however, the popularity of damselfly and dragonfly watching is catching up to butterfly watching, which in turn is slowly catching up to bird watching. If you've tried bird watching, and if you believe that mere mortals can actually identify sparrows and shorebirds in the field, then you may someday agree that the bluets are manageable, too.

LENGTH: about 32 mm.
HABITAT: widely distributed in ponds and lakes across B.C.

PACIFIC FORKTAIL
Ischnura cervula

With a name like "forktail," you'd think this bug would have, as they say, a forked tail—but no such luck. The male has a very tiny bump on the top of the tip of his abdomen that is about as well-forked as the humps on a Bactrian Camel. The shape of the fork is important for telling species apart, and that is probably why it was deemed so important.

Females are more difficult to tell apart, at least for people, but the damselflies have an interesting way of sorting each other out. On the very tip of his abdomen, the male has a set of claspers, which fit perfectly on the back of the female's neck. When a male tries to mate with a female, he first attempts to get her in a head-lock, so to speak. At this point, three things can happen. First, he can succeed, after which they fly away in tandem, mate and deposit the eggs. Second, the female may reject the male, and evade his claspers with a bit of damselfly judo. Or third, the male may find that his claspers don't quite fit, which may be a sign that he has accosted the wrong species of female, or worse, another male. After all, they are only damselflies—they are allowed to make mistakes.

> **LENGTH:** about 30 mm.
> **HABITAT:** ponds in the Interior, lower mainland and eastern Vancouver Island.

COMMON SPREADWING
Lestes disjunctus

These damselflies have only a bit of blue on them, right at the tip of the abdomen and again at the base of the wings. When they are young, they are iridescent green or brown, and as they get older they become covered in a waxy powder, like the "bloom" on a plum, leading damselfly specialists to call it "pruinosity," from the same root as "prune." The spreadwing damselflies are most common later in summer, when their pruinosity is fully developed.

Together, damselflies and dragonflies form the insect Order Odonata, and, unfortunately, we have no English term that refers to them both together. British people use the word "dragonfly" in this way, but it seems to me that giving "dragonfly" two confusingly similar meanings is a bad idea. I prefer the term "odonates" or just simply "odes" myself. Telling damselflies from dragonflies is easy—damselflies are thin, and all of their wings are similar in shape. Dragonflies are more heavily built, and the hind wings are broader than the front ones. Some people will tell you that damselflies always fold their wings over their backs, but obviously the spreadwings are an exception to this rule.

LENGTH: 35 mm.
HABITAT: widely distributed in ponds and lakes across B.C.

BLUE-EYED DARNER
Aeshna multicolor

The darners are our biggest dragonflies, and the Blue-eyed Darner is one of the most common of the darners. Up close, the male is a dark brown insect, patterned in blue and green, with sky blue eyes. Some of the females are coloured this way, while others are brown and yellow.

Darners spend most of the day on the wing, cruising the mid-summer skies for insects, which they capture in flight with their long, spiny legs. In turn, the darners are an important source of food for Merlin and American Kestrel falcons, and young falcons learn their hunting skills by chasing darners through the air. Darners breed in ponds and lakes, but they will also wander far from water to feed.

The name "darner," by the way, comes from the mistaken notion that these dragonflies will sew up your lips with their stinger. In reality, they have no stinger, and they don't sew, so put aside your fears. Some entomologists have suggested that this rumour got started when people wading in the shallows were accidentally jabbed by female darners, who were trying to lay eggs. I guess a bare leg is easy to mistake for a soft water plant. Darners are on the wing from late June all the way to the killing frosts of October.

> **LENGTH:** 70 mm.
> **HABITAT:** widespread in the southern parts of B.C.

PALE SNAKETAIL

Ophiogompus severus

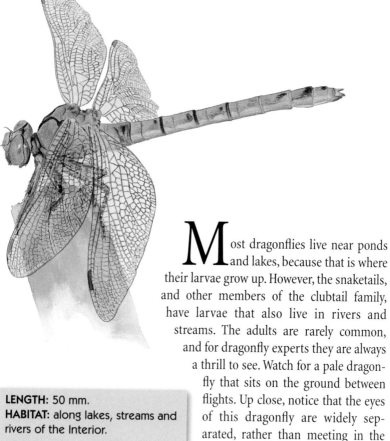

LENGTH: 50 mm.
HABITAT: along lakes, streams and rivers of the Interior.

Most dragonflies live near ponds and lakes, because that is where their larvae grow up. However, the snaketails, and other members of the clubtail family, have larvae that also live in rivers and streams. The adults are rarely common, and for dragonfly experts they are always a thrill to see. Watch for a pale dragonfly that sits on the ground between flights. Up close, notice that the eyes of this dragonfly are widely separated, rather than meeting in the middle of the head. Although the clubtail family is named for the expanded abdomen tips of some of its members, the snaketails have only a modest "club."

The Pale Snaketail is sometimes found along the valleys of the bigger Interior rivers in mid-summer. Notice that their coloration includes none of the intense blues and reds of other dragonflies. Instead, they are a light grass green. Green colour in animals is typically produced by a combination of yellow pigment and a blue "scattering" of light—the same thing that makes the sky blue. In other words, "Why is the sky blue" is a much simpler question than "Why is the snaketail green?"

AMERICAN EMERALD

Cordulia shurtleffi

W hat a fine dragonfly the American Emerald is! With gleaming green eyes and a jade black, iridescent body, it has a certain style all its own. The American Emerald is our most common member of the

LENGTH: 45 mm.
HABITAT: widely distributed in ponds and lakes across B.C.

emerald family, and it is a species of early summer. It's hard to say whether emeralds or clubtails generate more excitement among dragonfly enthusiasts, but it's probably safe to say that the clubtails rule in the south, while the emeralds are symbols of the great northern forests.

The American Emerald lays its eggs in ponds and small lakes, and that is probably why it is so common. Other sorts of emeralds prefer boggy pools deep in black spruce and tamarack peatlands or high mountain lakes, and these habitats contribute not only to their rarity but also to their appeal. To get a good look at any of the emeralds, it really does help to catch them. Crouching by a skinny little brook as it flows through the muskeg below a beaver pond, the "odonatist" waits. Mosquitoes swarm by the dozens, but the stalker dares not swat them for fear of spooking a passing dragonfly. When one finally comes in reach, one swing of the net is all it will allow, and with it you either bag the emerald or you do not.

HUDSONIAN WHITEFACE
Leucorrhinia hudsonica

This dragonfly is one of the first to emerge in spring. In warm years that means April, but when the weather is cool the first ones may not pop out until late May or even later in the north or at high elevations. The whiteface dragonflies are recognizable by a combination of a bright white face and a small, black splotch near the base of each hind wing. The rest of the body is boldly patterned in black and red (on mature males and some females) or black and yellow (on most females and young males). The bright contrasting colours are further enhanced by a coat of white hairs on the underside of the body.

These whitefaces are some of our smallest dragonflies, but they are also some of our most beautiful. In contrast to the meadowhawks (pp. 120–21) that emerge later in the year, whitefaces seem to spend more time around the ponds in which they breed. There, they perch on floating logs, scan the newly leafed shorelines for potential mates and sometimes wander out into clearings and along woodsy trails in the process. When the first mosquitoes of the year emerge, the whitefaces are their nemesis, but of course the dragonflies eat other insects as well, especially if they are abundant.

LENGTH: 30 mm.
HABITAT: widely distributed in B.C.

FOUR-SPOTTED SKIMMER

Libellula quadrimaculata

The name of this fine dragonfly proves one thing beyond any doubt—entomologists can't count. Because the wings on one side look just like the wings on the other, I guess they didn't bother looking for all eight black spots. If you count the black hind wing bases, there are really 10 spots, but at this point who cares? The Four-spotted Skimmer is a handsome animal, with a thick muscular body and a broad, streamlined abdomen. When it is in the prime of its life, its colours are vivid orange and black, but they do fade as the dragonfly gets older.

You see the Four-spotted Skimmer mostly around ponds and lakes, and it seems to like patrolling along the reedy shoreline. Females lay their eggs alone, by dipping their abdomen in the water while they fly. Males of many other dragonflies remain attached so no other male can interrupt the egg-laying process and mate with the female again. This species also lives

> **LENGTH:** 42 mm.
> **HABITAT:** widespread in ponds and lakes across B.C.

in Europe, where it is famous for its mass-migrations, which blacken the skies, or when it rests by the thousands on ocean-going ships. Too bad these migrations don't happen in B.C. as well.

CHERRY-FACED MEADOWHAWK

Sympetrum internum

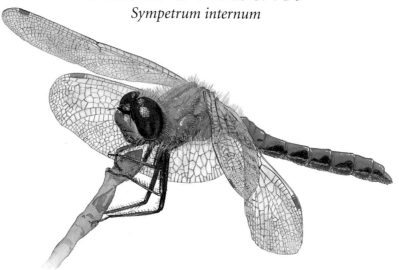

For most people, there are two "kinds" of dragonflies in B.C.—the big blue ones and the little red or yellow ones. The blue ones are, of course, the darners, while the red or yellow ones are the meadowhawks. Meadowhawks are about the same size as whitefaces (see p. 118), but they do not have a dark base on the hind wing, and most of them fly later in the season. The Cherry-faced Meadowhawk is one of our most common species. Males have a deep red body and a truly cherry red face. Females and young males are yellowish.

Unlike the whitefaces, the meadowhawks wander a great distance from their breeding ponds, and they show up in parks and gardens all the time. They like to perch on the ground, or on low vegetation, so you can usually sneak up on them to get a good look. In nearby Alberta, an unusual aspect of the behaviour of this dragonfly was first observed by a visiting bugster from Europe. He noticed that pairs of Cherry-faced Meadowhawks would fly low over lawns, dipping the female's abdomen to lay eggs. To the dragonflies, mowed lawns must look like places that flood in springtime, sure to provide habitat for their aquatic larvae.

LENGTH: 35 mm.
HABITAT: widespread near ponds and lakes across B.C.

BLACK MEADOWHAWK
Sympetrum danae

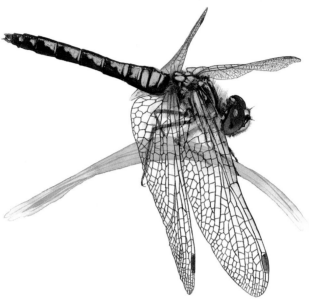

The Black Meadowhawk is another common meadowhawk species, and it is easy to recognize because the males are almost black once they mature. They are the only male meadowhawks with absolutely no red on them. Young ones, and females, are patterned in black and yellow, and they look a lot like female whitefaces. However, while the whitefaces emerge at the beginning of dragonfly season, the Black Meadowhawks first appear in mid-summer. They seem to live a long time, and often the last dragonflies of fall are Black Meadowhawks, hugging the ground for warmth with the sun sinking lower and lower in the sky.

LENGTH: 38 mm.
HABITAT: widely distributed in open areas in B.C.

Like the Four-spotted Skimmer (p. 119), this dragonfly is also found in Europe and northern Asia. They behave much like Cherry-faced Meadowhawks, but they are less likely to show up in your garden and less gullible when it comes to laying eggs in lawns (some other species can also be fooled into laying eggs on shiny cars!). The scientific name, by the way, means "Danae's Rock-lover." When you see a name that ends in *-i*, it generally refers to a man's name, while *-ae* refers to a woman (and Danae was a woman in Greek mythology). *Sym* means "loving," *petrum* means "rock."

SNOW FLEA
Family Isotomuridae

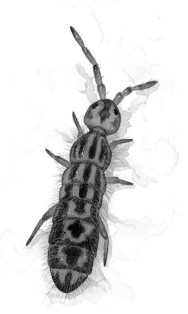

Snow Fleas are really springtails, and springtails are "really" either very primitive insects, or a group that is so primitive that they shouldn't be even considered insects. They never have wings, even as adults, and they are all tiny little dwellers in leaf litter and other moist places, where they are scavengers on decaying matter. Most people see representatives of this group, oddly enough, in winter time, when particular sorts of springtails come out on the snow during the mid-day warmth of pleasant winter afternoons.

LENGTH: up to 2 mm.
HABITAT: widely distributed across B.C.

With their amazing "tails," they leap about on the surface of the snow, obviously immune to the cold. The tail is actually an organ that comes out of the bottom of the springtail's abdomen, and it is used like a catapult to fling the bug up into the air. Most likely, they are not entirely pleased to be on the snow and are trying to get to someplace where the snow has melted, so they can go back to life the way they like it. It is possible that they do find things to eat on the snow, however, and if you have a good close look at the surface of partly melted snow you'll see it's not as clean as it looks from up high.

KAYAK POND SKATER

Limnoporus notabilis

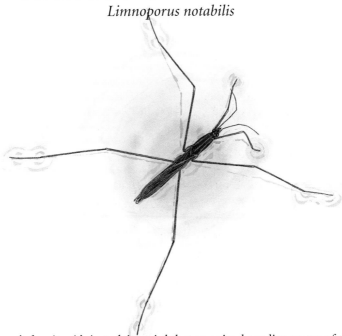

L et's face it—it's just plain weird that an animal can live on top of the water, without falling through, and pond skaters do so in a particularly fascinating way. Four very long legs support their slender body, and thus their wispy mass is distributed over a large area of the water's surface. The water itself has a sort of skin to it (the "surface tension") that is strong enough to support an insect, but only if its legs repel water, which naturally a pond skater's do. For these little bugs, the surface of a pond must feel like a great, slippery waterbed mattress, stretching off in all directions. On this bizarre playing field they search for food in the form of other bugs

LENGTH: up to 20 mm.
HABITAT: throughout B.C.

that have fallen in and drowned, or that are in the process of drowning.

Because pond skaters are sucking bugs, they have the same sort of piercing proboscis that allows their aquatic relatives to overpower and consume their own buggy prey. Kayak Pond Skaters have wings, but many of their relatives produce some adults that are wingless. Those pond skaters that are winged can leave the pond and settle elsewhere, while those that are wingless must be satisfied with their humble pool, and trust that things will remain to their liking.

GIANT WATER BUG
Lethocerus americanus

With its swollen forearms, this critter looks a bit like Arnold Schwarzenegger holding two long spikes above his head. Oddly enough, the Giant Water Bug also looks like a domino-sized piece of wet brown cardboard. In flight, it looks a lot like a small bat, and it is often attracted to lights at night.

Once this bug grasps a luckless fish, tadpole or fellow insect, the result is inevitable: the sucking beak plunges deep, and digestive juices are injected. Because of these juices, the prey dissolves inside its own body, while the willow leaf–sized insect holds on and waits until the time is right to suck.

LENGTH: 50 mm.
HABITAT: ponds and lakes throughout B.C.

When the meal is done, the bug swims off to digest, using two pairs of swimming legs, not one. After all, it is our largest aquatic insect, and it needs the extra power to propel its hefty body through the water. Young Giant Water Bugs look much like the adults but without wings. These impressive creatures can be found in still or slow-flowing waters, and they are most abundant in cattail marshes. And yes, if one bites you, it really does hurt.

WATER BOATMAN
Family Corixidae

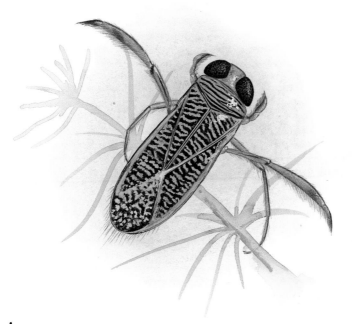

Although small, water boatmen are amazing. Take a look at their legs. The first pair are shaped like little garden trowels, and the bug uses them for sifting through muck for food. The next pair are long and pointed, and the boatman uses them to hold onto plants or rocks while under water. Then there are the back legs, which are the boatman's oars.

If you keep a water boatman in a glass jar, you can see how it breathes under water. A layer of air clings to the boatman's tummy, and it breathes from this bubble. The oxygen the bug needs enters the bubble from the surrounding water. At the same time, carbon dioxide leaves the bubble and goes into the pond. Slowly, the bubble gets smaller as nitrogen goes into the water, and then the bug pops to the surface to replenish its air supply.

LENGTH: 4–10 mm.
HABITAT: fresh-water habitats throughout B.C.

Water boatmen live in ponds, rivers, lakes and even saline sloughs. At times, millions of them can be in one place, and so many of them may accidentally fly to lights at night that they can cover the ground.

COMMON BACKSWIMMER
Notonecta undulata

Are you any good at the back-stroke? Well, it seems that the back-swimmer doesn't know any other way to swim. At first, you might think that a backswimmer is just an upside-down water boatman but have another look. Both pairs of front legs are short and stocky, for grabbing prey, and instead of resting on under-water plants, backswimmers lounge right at the top of the pond. They rest with their legs touching the underside of the water surface and their heads aimed slightly downward, ready to dive.

LENGTH: 11 mm.
HABITAT: throughout B.C.

If you catch one and flip it over, you'll see how pretty it is, with bright white wings and fiery red eyes. Don't let it bite you though! The bite of a backswimmer is like that of a Giant Water Bug (p. 124)—intended to dissolve the flesh of their prey.

People who keep fish in outdoor ponds dread backswimmers, because they eat a lot of small fishes, as well as other bugs. In nature, however, they are both the predator and the prey, and they make the world of the pond more interesting, even if it is a bit more dangerous. Although backswimmers are predators themselves, they live in fear of such things as Giant Water Bugs, diving beetles and bigger fishes, too.

ACILIUS DIVING BEETLE
Acilius semisulcatus

Most water bugs and water beetles float, whether they want to or not. While they swim, you can see how they fight to stay down in the water, and how they drift up to the top the moment they quit paddling. Not so with the Acilius Diving Beetle. It seems to be able to match its buoyancy to the water around it. This creature is super streamlined, and it slips through the water like a polished pumpkin seed, making it one of the most graceful swimmers in the insect world.

You mostly find these beetles in natural ponds, rather than in the sorts of meltwater ponds that form in

LENGTH: 13 mm.
HABITAT: ponds and lakes throughout B.C.

parks and schoolyards in spring. They are not rare, but they are always exciting to catch. You can recognize one by the half-moon markings on the tips of its wing covers, and by the snappy yellow slash on the pronotum shield behind the beetle's head. Like Giant Diving Beetles (p. 129), male Acilius Diving Beetles have round sucker pads on their front feet, to help them hold onto the slippery females while they mate.

WATER SCORPION
Ranatra fusca

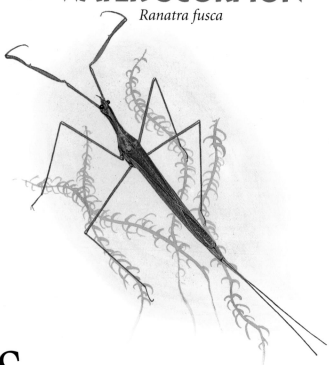

Structurally, a Water Scorpion is built almost exactly like a Giant Water Bug (p. 124) but on a much slimmer plan. To look at it, however, you'd think you were gazing at an underwater praying mantid. Water Scorpions do indeed catch their buggy prey with their forelegs, the way mantids do (p. 108), but their forelegs are not spiked, and their heads do not turn to look at things all around them. As well, they have piercing, sucking mouthparts, not the chewing mouthparts of mantids. Amazingly, they can get up out of the water and fly to a new pond when the need arises. Or at least the adults can—young Water Scorpions look much like their parents but without wings.

LENGTH: up to 30 mm, not counting the breathing tube.
HABITAT: ponds and lakes in southern B.C.

Water Scorpions breathe through a siphon that extends out the back of their abdomens. The siphon is not a tube but rather two parallel rods of cuticle with water-repellent hairs on them. Because the surface tension of the water cannot penetrate the hairs, the siphon acts like a tube even though it is not solid.

GIANT DIVING BEETLES
Dytiscus spp.

Next to the Giant Water Bug (p. 124), and some really big dragonfly larvae, this diving beetle is our biggest aquatic insect. It, too, is a powerful predator that will eat almost anything it can overpower. If you keep pond critters in an aquarium, you will find that sooner or later there is only one left, and in most cases the survivor will be either a Giant Water Bug or a Giant Diving Beetle.

The Alaskan Giant Diving Beetle (*D. alaskanus*) is probably our most common species, but it is also one of the smallest of the giants. The most impressive member of this group is the Harris's Diving Beetle (*D. harrisii*)— a big one can be 40 mm long! Female giant diving beetles come in two forms, in most species. The first form looks a lot like the male, with shiny, black wing covers. The second form has grooves running the length of the wing covers, making it look, at first glance, like it must be a different species. A female with a white blob on the end of her abdomen has been mated; the white stuff discourages other males from mating with her again. Males have round sucker pads on their front feet, for holding onto the females.

LENGTH: 27 mm.
HABITAT: almost any freshwater throughout B.C.

If you notice a bad smell when handling these beetles, it is probably their defence chemicals. These steroids are powerful, and predators respect them.

WHIRLIGIG BEETLE
Gyrinus spp.

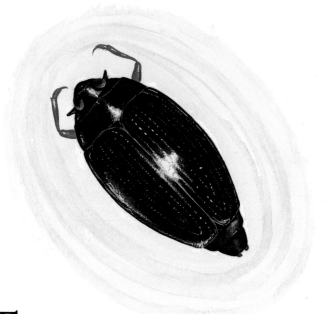

This water beetle is probably the coolest of them all. With the most efficient swimming legs in the entire animal world, it zips around on top of the water spinning and whirling like a super-fast bumper car. If it needs to, it can dive under water like a diving beetle, and it also has wings when the time comes to find a new pond. Sometimes, dozens of these water beetles band together to form a flotilla on the surface.

If you have a microscope, and a whirligig specimen, you can see how amazing its eyes are. Each eye is actually split in two! One half looks up into the air, while the other half watches down into the water. Of course, while Whirligig Beetles are spinning and whirling at high speed, their eyes need all the help they can get, so they also use their short triangular antennae to "feel" their way through the twists and turns.

LENGTH: 4–6 mm.
HABITAT: ponds and lakes throughout B.C.

Whirligig Beetles are predators, and they will eat any unfortunate bug they can catch on the water's surface. Even baby water striders are not fast enough to get away from them. And if another animal tries to eat a whirligig, it gets a mouthful of something that smells a lot like rotting fruit.

GIANT WATER SCAVENGER BEETLE

Hydrophilus triangularis

Finally, a water beetle that isn't a ferocious predator! Water scavengers are the gentle ones in the water beetle crowd, and they feed on plants and various sorts of debris. When they swim, they paddle like crazy with all six legs, and most of the time they cling to underwater plants. In many ways, they look like they are trying to pretend they are not under water at all, like leaf beetles on the willows by the shore.

Whereas the diving beetles (p. 129) keep their air supply under their wings, hidden from view, the water scavengers keep air both under the wings and all along their undersides. Under water, they look like they are coated with liquid mercury. To replenish the bubble, they don't just bob to the surface either. Instead, they barely stick their head up, and let the air flow in around their antennae. For water scavengers, life is careful and slow. For diving beetles, it is risky and fast. This species is the biggest water scavenger beetle in North America. Smaller types abound, mind you, and the large ones are certainly not typical of their family (Hydrophilidae).

LENGTH: 35 mm.
HABITAT: ponds and lakes in southern B.C.

DAMSELFLY LARVA

Lestes spp.

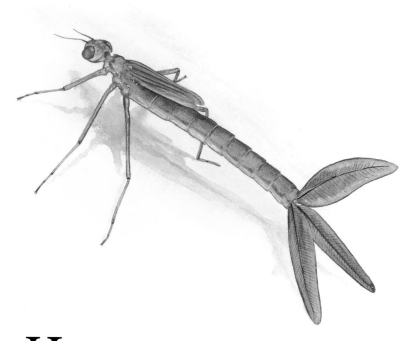

Here's an odd critter. At the back end of its long, slender body, you see three things that look like dead leaves. These "leaves" are the insect's gills, by which it takes oxygen from the water. Six long legs help it scramble among the underwater plants, where it watches for prey with its bulging compound eyes. When a small edible insect is spotted, the larva takes aim and suddenly the folded lower lip shoots out, many times the length of the larva's head. The lower lip grabs the unlucky prey like the tongue of a chameleon lizard.

LENGTH: up to 29 mm.
HABITAT: throughout B.C.

Damselfly larvae are common in ponds and lakes, and they are easy to recognize. They are not good swimmers, mind you, and when they do have to swim, they wiggle through the water like a person with their hands at their sides. If you look closely at the top of a damselfly larva's thorax, you'll see four little wing pads. These wing pads will eventually become the adult damselfly's wings, when the larva finally climbs up out of the water and sheds its skin for the final time.

DRAGONFLY LARVA

Aeshna spp.

Damselfly larvae are weird, but dragonfly larvae are even weirder. Both have the folding lower lip that catches prey, and both have big eyes and slender legs, but there the similarities seem to end. Dragonfly larvae are bigger, heavier and more powerful than damselfly larvae. As well, instead of leaf-like gills, they keep their gills inside the end of their abdomen, in their rectum. That means, I'm afraid, that they breathe with their butt. And when they need to swim, what do they do? They squirt water out their back end, and shoot through the pond with jet propulsion.

LENGTH: up to 47 mm.
HABITAT: ponds and lakes throughout B.C.

The larvae of dragonflies are long and streamlined, like the illustration shown here. Skimmer dragonfly larvae have longer legs and fatter bodies, sometimes with lots of spikes out the sides. Often, they become covered with algae and pond "guck." Perhaps the oddest dragonfly larvae are the snaketails (p. 116), which spend their lives partly buried in mud at the bottom of streams and rivers and have smaller eyes and shorter legs. No matter what the species, dragonfly larvae take at least a few months to grow up, and when they emerge to become adults, they crawl up on plants or on the sandy banks of rivers.

WATER TIGER
Dytiscus spp.

The Water Tiger is really just the larva of the Giant Diving Beetle (p. 129), and other sorts of diving beetles have similar larvae, too. This larva's name leads some people to confuse the diving beetles and the tiger beetles, but tiger beetles only live on land and never in the water.

A Water Tiger is a marvellous beast. It swims with all six legs and in a very graceful fashion, floating almost effortlessly through the pond. On its broad, flat head, the Water Tiger has eyes, but they are simple eyes, not the large compound eyes of the adults. As well, whereas an adult kills its prey by chewing on it with short but powerful jaws, the jaws of the Water Tiger are like two hypodermic needles. The Water Tiger swims up to its prey, and then attacks quickly and savagely. Once the fish or tadpole has been impaled, digestive juices are injected, and the prey dissolves in its own body. You might think this manner of attack would make Water Tigers some of the most fearsome creatures in the pond, but they often fall prey to both Giant Water Bugs (p. 124) and the adults of their own species. Most Water Tigers prefer to eat small vertebrates, but some are more fond of eating insects instead. Like the adults, Water Tigers must come to the surface to breathe, and their breathing hole is located right at the tip of their abdomen.

LENGTH: up to 60 mm.
HABITAT: ponds and lakes throughout B.C.

CADDISFLY LARVA
Order Trichoptera

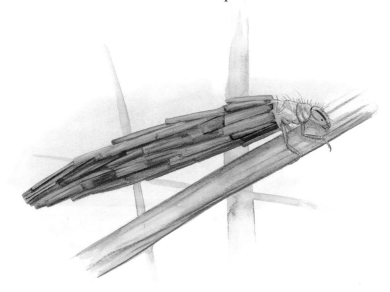

To most people, an adult caddisfly doesn't quite qualify as a "cool" bug. It is mothlike and only moderately colourful, and the only obvious things that set it apart from other bugs is its wispy, long antennae. But every caddisfly was once a larva, and caddisfly larvae are just plain nifty. Most caddisfly larvae are scavengers, but some eat algae, which they graze from rocks and water plants. While the larvae are grazing, they are constantly at risk from all of the underwater predators around them. So they protect themselves with cases—coverings for their soft, grublike bodies. Some of these larvae make the cases from twigs, while others use pebbles, reeds or leaves, held together with silk and saliva. Most of cases are straight, but some are coiled like a snail shell. Some larvae don't make cases at all.

LENGTH: with case, up to 60 mm.
HABITAT: ponds and lakes throughout B.C.

To find caddisfly larvae, look into a shallow pond, and watch the bottom. Pretty soon, you'll see things move that you thought were just debris, but instead they are the larval cases. Trout eat many of these insects, by the way, and experiments have shown that they recognize Caddisfly Larvae by looking for their eyes. "If it has eyes, it must be alive" is the trout's rule, and when you think of it, that's not a bad way to find bugs yourself.

GIANT STONEFLY (SALMONFLY) LARVA

Pteronarcys spp.

At first the larva of a Giant Stonefly might look a lot like a great big Mayfly Larva (p. 137), but look closely and notice the differences. Salmonflies are a type of stonefly, and stoneflies form an insect order separate from the mayflies. A stonefly larva has only two long feelers on the end of its abdomen, whereas a mayfly usually has three. The stonefly larva will keep this feature as an adult, and, in fact, an adult stonefly looks a whole lot like a larva, except with wings. When the biggest of our stoneflies emerge as adults, fishermen call them "Salmonflies" and trout go wild trying to eat as many as possible while the feast lasts.

LENGTH: up to 50 mm.
HABITAT: rivers and streams throughout B.C.

Stoneflies don't live in ponds or lakes—they only like streams and rivers. Even then, they seem to prefer clear, fast-flowing water, with lots of dissolved oxygen. Unlike Mayfly Larvae, with gills on the sides of their abdomens, stonefly larva gills are tucked into their leg pits, so to speak. Without a powerful magnifying glass, and with an upside-down larva, the gills are tough to see.

What do stonefly larvae eat? Mostly they eat water plants and algae, much like Caddisfly Larvae (p. 135) and water scavenger beetles (p. 131), but some are predators. With their powerful legs, they hold onto underwater rocks, and fight the current that threatens to sweep them away.

MAYFLY LARVA
Order Ephemeroptera

Some kinds of bugs seem to exist only for the sake of getting eaten by other creatures, which, of course, isn't true. It just seems that way sometimes. Mayflies and their larvae are one such group, and they are about as defenceless as bugs can get.

The one illustrated here is part of a group of Mayfly Larvae called "crawlers." The other 100–200 species of mayflies in this part of the world are either crawlers, burrowers or swimmers. Each one has its own style of feeding, and they all eat things like algae and detritus. Some of these species even sieve food from the water, with their hairy front feet.

LENGTH: up to 30 mm.
HABITAT: fresh-water habitats throughout B.C.

Some Mayfly Larvae live in streams, some in ponds, some in lakes and some in rivers. The easiest way to recognize them is by their three-pronged abdomen tip, and the fuzzy gills that line the sides of their abdomen.

When mayflies emerge as adults, they generally live only a single day. At first they are called "duns" or "subimagos"—an odd stage that no other insect goes through. Then they shed their skin again, wings and all, and become the short-lived true adult that lives only long enough to mate and lay eggs.

SOW BUG

Oniscus aselus

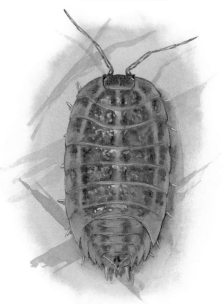

In general, insects are the bugs of the land, while crustaceans are the bugs of the sea. Some crustaceans, however, do live on land, although they need moist places to survive (they breathe with modified gills). Remember, crabs are also crustaceans, and we have all seen the air-breathing hermit crabs that are such popular critters in pet stores. Even sea-shore crabs can spend a fair amount of time out of the water, up on rocks or sand.

Sow Bugs were accidentally introduced from—where else?—Europe. It is interesting that European bugs generally do well when they are introduced to North America but not the other way around. Sow Bugs are sometimes confused with Pill Bugs (*Armadillidium vulgare*), but Pill Bugs roll up into a ball when they are frightened, and Sow Bugs do not. Sow Bugs are all slow-moving, heavily armoured creatures that are easily recognized by their many legs and their many-segmented shell of a body. They are not harmful, and they feed only on decaying material, both plant and animal. Because our gardens are almost completely unnatural ecosystems to begin with, the addition of Sow Bugs is not much different from adding another species of non-native flowering plant.

> **LENGTH:** about 10 mm.
> **HABITAT:** gardens and similar areas in southern B.C.

GARDEN CENTIPEDE
Lithobius sp.

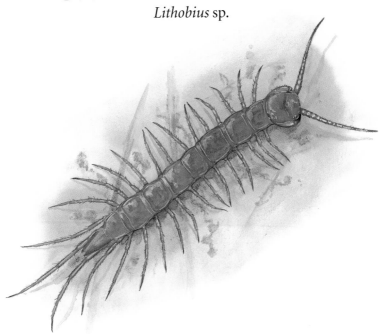

L ift a board, or turn the soil in your average B.C. garden, and you're likely to find a centipede. The typical specimen is about 25 mm long and rusty orange in colour. Centipedes move rapidly, twist like miniature snakes and can squeeze into what seems like the tiniest of openings to escape your prying eyes. These abilities are probably why you also find them in basements so often. A slight opening between a window and the foundation, or a crack between wood and cement, will allow them to get in.

Once in the house, however, they are no longer in contact with their most cherished substance—moisture. They quickly dry out indoors,

LENGTH: up to about 30 mm.
HABITAT: gardens and moist forests throughout B.C.

and usually when you find them, they are desiccated and shrivelled to about half their normal size. Centipedes are predators, and they have venomous fangs that they use to subdue their prey. Our B.C. species are not dangerous to people, but small children should still avoid handling them. If you can get one to sit still for a moment, you'll see that each body segment carries one pair of legs, and the legs are set off to the sides. On a millipede, each segment bears two legs, which are set underneath.

CYANIDE MILLIPEDE

Harpaphe haydeniana

The main similarity between a millipede and a centipede is that both their names end in "-pede," a word root that refers to their feet. Millipedes are slow-moving animals that feed on plants or detritus. Big millipedes, at least in this part of the world, are bigger than big centipedes. The Cyanide Millipede is noteworthy because it does indeed produce cyanide as a defensive chemical. Some people call it the "almond-scented millipede," however, I say let's be honest about the smell—the scent really comes from cyanide, not almonds.

Millipedes have many more legs than a centipede, because there are two pairs of legs per segment. There are so many legs that these legs run the risk of getting in each other's way. So, the millipede moves its legs in slow, coordinated waves, starting at the back of the body and moving toward the head. Speaking of which, the antennae on a millipede's head give this creature a somewhat insect-like appearance from the neck forward, and, indeed, the science of animal classification places millipedes closer to insects than centipedes.

LENGTH: about 45 mm.
HABITAT: forested areas of southern coastal B.C.

For those who know that millipede means "1000 foot" while centipede means "100 foot," please make a note that millipedes always have fewer than a 1000 feet, and centipedes can have as few as 30 feet. A 100-footed centipede is actually an impossibility—they always have an odd number of leg pairs, giving either $49 \times 2 = 98$ or $51 \times 2 = 102$ legs in total.

NORTHERN SCORPION

Paruroctonus boreus

Scorpions are tropical creatures, right? So what are they doing in B.C.? Well, they do like warmth, so the only places you can find them here are on bare, sun-facing hillsides in the dry southern regions of the Okanagan, around Osoyoos and Penticton and down to the U.S. border. The Northern Scorpion is, in fact, the most northerly species of scorpion in North America.

Scorpions are unmistakable, with their pincer claws, eight walking legs and long abdomen with a sting at the end. Some scorpions from much farther south can be deadly venomous. The Northern Scorpion's sting, however, is apparently not much worse than a hornet's. Mind you, reports of the

LENGTH: 35 mm.
HABITAT: dry open areas in the southern Okanagan.

effect of a Northern Scorpion sting are few, and it's best not to take chances. Even if you spend time in a scorpion's habitat, you will probably have trouble finding it. By day scorpions stay under rocks. By night they hunt on the ground for other small bugs, and then you can find them with a flashlight. If you have one, try putting "black light" bulbs in a portable fluorescent camping light. Under the rays of ultraviolet light, scorpions glow with an eerie green colour, making them much easier to spot. Remember though, these animals are rare here, so treat them with kindness and respect, and let them go back to their business.

NORTHERN CAMEL SPIDER
Eremobates gladiolus

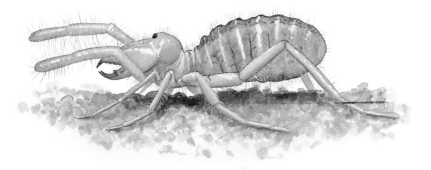

It would be unfair to characterize this arachnid as a psychopathic killer, but hey, that's what they look like to most of the people who have encountered one. These oddball critters have a horrific combination of spiderish legs, a thin-walled bulbous abdomen, a bit of hairiness and a front end that is made up almost entirely of jaw-like pincers. These pincers are held in an up-and-down fashion, rather than side-to-side like most other bugs, and they make camel spiders look horrifically mammal-like when they chew. Their speckish eyes give no sense of intelligence whatsoever, and, indeed, camel spiders live mainly to kill other bugs.

LENGTH: about 20 mm.
HABITAT: dry areas in the southern Okanagan.

I suppose they also live to reproduce, and to their credit the mother camel spider guards her eggs for many weeks, and stays with the young until they complete their first moult. These spiders can be found in the same sorts of hot, dry habitats as scorpions, and Osoyoos is the camel spider capital of B.C. "Windscorpions," "solifuges," "camel spiders" and "sunspiders" are some of the names these arachnids are called. I prefer "camel spider," the Arabian name, because we once had native camels in this part of the world, and these bugs watched the rise and fall of the North American camel era, long before the arrival of humans. As well, prominent specialists on this group seem to have settled on the name "camel spider" as well.

HARVESTMAN
Order Opiliones

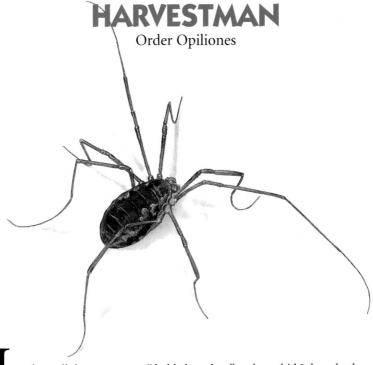

I used to call these creatures "daddy long-legs" and as a kid I thought they were spiders. I now try to use the more traditional name "Harvestman" to refer to them, because just about any long-legged bug gets called "daddy long-legs." Harvestmen are not spiders—spiders have two main body parts while Harvestmen have no constriction between the head and the abdomen. Harvestmen are also unable to produce silk, and they have no poison glands. Their two eyes are set in a little mound on top of the body, and the eight legs extend out from the sides.

These critters are predatory, although as you might imagine they are no match for anything but small prey. They will also scavenge on dead bugs or bits of decaying plants. Because they are such familiar garden bugs, various odd beliefs have developed about them. Some people believe that they are extremely venomous, even though it is tough to get them to bite. This story is, as far as I can determine, complete baloney. Another weird story has to do with the belief that if your cow goes missing, you pull off a Harvestman's leg and throw it on the ground, where it will point you in the right direction.

LENGTH: about 5 mm, without the legs.
HABITAT: forests and gardens throughout B.C.

143

ROCKY MOUNTAIN WOOD TICK
Dermacentor andersoni

Here's an unpopular "bug." To find one, take a walk in cattle country late in spring or early in summer. Make sure to tramp through some long grasses and some low shrubs, where ticks might be waiting to grab on to a passing "host." Then, before you go to sleep, take off your clothes and do a "tick check." Use a mirror for those tricky places you can't see. If you're lucky, the little things will still be walking around, looking for a place to plunge their mouthparts. If not, you have to pull them out, very slowly and carefully, with forceps near the head, because you don't want to leave the mouthparts in your skin.

LENGTH: about 5 mm.
HABITAT: shrubby areas in the Interior.

Most of the time, a tick bite is of no consequence, but east of the Rocky Mountains ticks can carry Rocky Mountain Spotted Fever, and they may carry Lyme Disease here as well. An even more rare condition occurs when a tick bites at the base of the skull, and the unlucky victim develops "tick paralysis." Fortunately, all it takes to cure this problem is to pull out the tick.

WOLF SPIDER
Family Lycosidae

Wolf Spiders are wandering hunters, and although they do not spin a web, they can still produce silk from the "spinneret" glands on their abdomen. Most of the time, you will see them in grassy places, where they search for other bugs. They are easy to find day or night, and if you search for them with a head lamp (not a flashlight), you'll see their eyes gleaming in the grass, like little points of dew. The trick is to go out looking on a dry night, when there is no dew to confuse you!

LENGTH: up to 10 mm.
HABITAT: open areas throughout B.C.

Wolf Spiders have moderately good vision, and they can also see the patterns of polarized light in the sky, helping them find their way around their grassy little worlds. Females are bigger than the males, and when they lay eggs, they wrap them in a silk bag. The bag is then attached to the spinnerets, and the female spider carries the eggs with her until they hatch. Carrying the eggs makes her resemble even bigger spiders with blue or off-white abdomens (the blue or off-white part being, of course, the egg sac). When the young hatch, they cling to the body of the mother, holding onto special handle hairs on her back.

145

BOREAL JUMPING SPIDER

Phidippus borealis

E ven those of us with a deep-seated fear of spiders sometimes see a glimmer of cuteness in the members of the jumping spider family. Sure, they have eight legs and eight eyes, but they don't move in the same creepy way that other spiders do. Instead, they walk around in a more insect-like fashion (if you know what I mean), and they also jump. When you look at one up close, most of the time it will turn and look back, with a pair of big, bright eyes on the front of its head.

LENGTH: up to 10 mm.
HABITAT: drier areas throughout B.C.

Jumping spiders have the best vision of any spider, and they can swivel their head around to examine whatever catches their interest. Add to these features the fact that some, like the Boreal Jumping Spider, have colourful bodies and iridescent fangs, and you have a spider with both a "face" and a personality. Many of the smaller jumping spiders also do complicated little courtship dances, waving their fangs, their palps (the little leggish things in front of the fangs) and their front legs, like coloured flags. If the female likes the dance, they will mate. Jumping spiders are not aggressive, but the bite of the biggest ones (in the genus *Phidippus*) can be painful and unsightly.

146

ORB-WEAVER

Aranaeus spp.

These spider make the classic "orb" webs that we all know and love—flat with radiating spokes and a spiral of silk connecting them together. If you have never watched a spider make a web, you really owe it to yourself to do so. If nothing else, it is fascinating to think of how wondrous it is that any animal could do something so complex based on nothing but pre-programmed instinct. As one of the few animals with almost no innate behaviour patterns (except perhaps things like smiling or yawning), we really can't imagine what it is like. The spider spins a perfect web every

LENGTH: up to 11 mm.
HABITAT: forests throughout B.C.

time, and knows exactly how to get around on it, holding the non-sticky threads while the prey get caught in the sticky ones.

Tossing small insects into an Orb-weaver's web is standard practice for outdoor kids, and we've all seen the spider wrap up its prey in silk and then deliver the death-fanging that injects the poison. These spiders also show us how easy it is for the average person to completely ignore an interesting sort of "bug"—only when they grow to full size do people notice them, and every entomologist gets phone calls every fall asking "What IS this thing?!"

LONG-JAWED ORB-WEAVER
Tetragnatha spp.

Oddly enough, in this part of the world there are two families of spiders that make orb webs. One family is made up of spiders that are plump and round, while the other family is made up of spiders that are long and slender. The latter group is called the Long-jawed Orb-weavers, and they are just as common as the regular orb-weavers, especially in wet meadows. In mid-summer, an area at dawn can be literally festooned with dewy cob webs, hanging heavy in the cool morning air.

With their slender bodies, these spiders are harder to see when they sit in the middle of their snares, which they do much of the time. They also hold their front four legs together in front of the head, and the hind four together behind the abdomen, to further break up their spiderish outline. Apart from their differences in body shape, the two groups of spiders have similar habits, and in both groups the males are smaller than the females and much more rarely seen. The family of Long-jawed Orb-weavers is named for the enlarged fangs. When these orb-weavers mate, the male and female hold each other by the jaws—probably the safest way to go about the matter.

LENGTH: about 10–15 mm.
HABITAT: grassy areas throughout B.C.

GIANT HOUSE SPIDER
Tegenaria gigantea

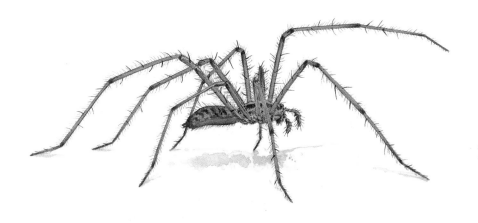

Back in the good old days of damp, drafty basements, the only spiders you were likely to find in your house were the usual, secretive cob-web builders. Or, you might see Wolf Spiders (p. 145) that wandered in from outside and got trapped by the slippery sides of the sink or the bathtub (leading to the silly belief that they "come up through the drains"). Nowadays, things are a bit more exciting, thanks to three species of introduced house spiders from Europe.

The most common is the Barn Funnel Weaver (*T. domestica*) that builds a sheet-like web in a dark corner of the basement. Then there is the Hobo Spider (*T. agrestis*), which can

LENGTH: leg span up to 8 cm.
HABITAT: centred on the major cities, but easily spread when people move.

cause an alarmingly ugly bite (it is the only dangerous member of the group, if that's any consolation). And finally, there is the Giant House Spider, which is, quite frankly, the creepiest bug in the whole darn province of B.C. When a long-legged male goes running across the floor of the rumpus room, all eight legs flailing like mad, it is no wonder that most people panic and call the exterminators.

SIX-SPOTTED FISHING SPIDER

Dolomedes triton

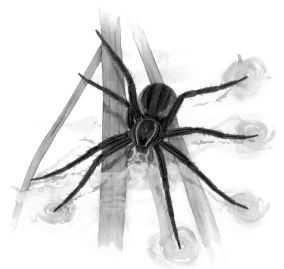

I f you read a lot of nature books, you'll eventually see pictures of these spiders eating small fishes. The spiders live in ponds and can walk on the water like a water strider, although they let their heavy bellies lay on the surface because they can't quite support their weight on tiptoes. They can crawl around on underwater plants, breathing from air trapped in the tiny hairs that cover their bodies and legs. So it is quite natural that they would eat small fishes. However, I once worked in a lab where we studied these spiders, and none of the arachnologists I worked with ever saw one get a fish! They ate lots of water striders, damselflies and bugs that fell in the water but no fishes. So maybe it happens more often in other places, or maybe those photographs were posed.

LENGTH: females to 15 mm, males to 10 mm.
HABITAT: ponds throughout B.C.

Female fishing spiders are bigger than the males, and often eat the males during or after courtship. Females who have already mated have less patience with suitors, so males sometimes follow immature females, waiting for them to reach adulthood. When the female lays her eggs, she carries them in a silk bag in her jaws, unlike female Wolf Spiders (p. 145), which carry the eggs on their spinnerets.

WESTERN BLACK WIDOW
Latrodectus hesperus

Black widows in B.C.? Absolutely! However, they are much easier to find in the Okanagan than elsewhere. The best way to see one is to walk around in mid-summer, and shine a flashlight down old mammal burrows. Usually, these black widows are easy to find. The black widow spins a disorganized web and is just about the easiest spider in B.C. to identify: shiny black with a red hourglass (or two red triangles) on its tummy.

The venom of these beasts can indeed be deadly, but fortunately these spiders are shy and docile most of the time. Females do eat the males quite often after mating, but this practice is actually fairly common among spiders, and it is not the macabre ritual that some people imagine. Apart from mammal burrows, the best place to look for black widows is in the grocery store—many of them come in with fruits and vegetables. Sometimes they have red or orange markings on their backs, indicating they are from the southern states. And if you see a smaller spider with a smudgy orange-brown mark on its tummy, don't be fooled. It is the Boreal Cobweb Spider (*Steatoda borealis*).

LENGTH: females to 12 mm, males to 5 mm.
HABITAT: dry areas in southern B.C.

GOLDENROD CRAB SPIDER

Misumena vatia

Here's the scenario: a big fat spider waits patiently in a fresh blossom. Sometimes the spider is yellow, and sometimes it is white. Sometimes these colours blend in perfectly with the flowers, while other times they don't. An insect comes to the flower for a sip of nectar, and suddenly it becomes spider fodder.

My favourite story about this spider involved a butterfly, a Western Tailed Blue. The blue was flitting about in the greenery, stopping from time to time to sun itself, when it spied another blue. It flapped over to investigate, but the second butterfly seemed completely uninterested. That's when I saw the female Goldenrod Crab Spider, tucked up between the purple flowers of the vetch they were all on. Before the first blue could comprehend the situation (if ever it could at all), the spider reached out, grabbed it and had two blues for lunch instead of one. Not only had the spider used the flower as an ambush, it also used the first blue as a decoy!

LENGTH: females about 8 mm, males about 3 mm.
HABITAT: meadows and clearings throughout B.C.

Males of this species are smaller than the females and are darker in colour. In a wild rose, they look almost exactly like the pollen-bearing stamens—the best buggy camouflage I know of in B.C.

BOOKS FOR BUGSTERS

Unlike birds or mammals, there is no one "book" that covers the entire bug fauna of B.C. or any other state, province or country for that matter. You must be ready to face the fact that we have a great deal of knowledge about a few selected groups of bugs and almost no knowledge of all the others.

It is sad that almost all the references that follow are out of print or hard to find. Hopefully, we will soon see an improvement in the funding and support that "faunistic" studies receive, and that the work of detailing our arthropod fauna grows more vibrant in the new millennium—whether it is led by amateurs or professionals, or people like me, on the border between.

The following books will take you a few steps further in your understanding of local bugs. I have avoided isolated papers in entomological journals, but if you are serious in your quest, these references will quickly lead you to them as well. I should also mention two important series of books. The first is entitled "Insects and Arachnids of Canada," and it was published by Agriculture Canada in Ottawa. It covers some of the spiders, beetles, two-winged flies and sucking bugs. Unfortunately, this series lost its funding before treating the entire Canadian fauna. The second is "The Moths of America North of Mexico, Including Greenland," and it is published by E.W. Classey Ltd. and R.B.D. Publications. It does not yet cover all of our moths, but the plan is to eventually treat each and every species.

You can also search the worldwide web for information on specific sorts of bugs. Some of it is well-researched and helpful, while most is not. Some groups, such as dragonflies, enjoy much better coverage on the web than others.

Books

Arnett, Ross H., Jr. 1985. *American Insects: A Handbook of the Insects of America North of Mexico.* Van Nostrand Reinhold Company, New York.

Bartlett Wright, Amy. 1993. *Peterson First Guide to Caterpillars of North America.* Houghton Mifflin Co., Boston and New York.

Bousquet, Yves, editor. 1991. *Checklist of Beetles of Canada and Alaska.* Agriculture Canada, Ottawa.

Cannings, Robert A., and Kathleen M. Stuart. 1977. *The Dragonflies of British Columbia.* British Columbia Provincial Museum, Handbook No. 35.

Cannings, Richard, and Sydney Cannings. 1996. *British Columbia, A Natural History.* Greystone Books, Douglas and McIntyre, Vancouver/Toronto.

Chu, H. F., and Laurence K. Cutkomp. 1992. *How to Know the Immature Insects.* Pictured Key Nature Series. Wm. C. Brown Publishers, Dubuque.

Danks, Hugh V., editor. 1978. *Canada and Its Insect Fauna.* Memoirs of the Entomological Society of Canada, No. 108.

Furniss, R.L., and V.M. Carolin. 1977. *Western Forest Insects.* U.S. Department of Agriculture, Forest Service. Miscellaneous Publications, No. 1339.

Gordon, Robert. 1985. *The Coccinellidae (Coleoptera) of North America North of Mexico.* Journal of the New York Entomological Society, Volume 93, No. 1.

Hatch, Melvin H. 1953–1971. *The Beetles of the Pacific Northwest. Parts I–V.* University of Washington Press, Seattle.

Holland, W.J. 1968. *The Moth Book.* Dover Publications Inc., New York.

Jaques, H.E. 1951. *How to Know the Beetles.* Wm. C. Brown Publishers, Dubuque.

Kaston, B.J. 1978. *How to Know the Spiders.* Pictured Key Nature Series. Wm. C. Brown Publishers, Dubuque.

Layberry, Ross, Peter W. Hall and J. Donald Lafontaine. 1998. *The Butterflies of Canada.* University of Toronto Press.

Lindroth, Carl H. 1961–1969. *The Ground-beetles of Canada and Alaska.* Opuscula Entomologica Supplementa XX, XXIV, XXIX, XXXIII, XXXIV and XXXV.

Opler, Paul A., and Amy Bartlett Wright. 1999. *A Field Guide to Western Butterflies.* Peterson Field Guide Series, Houghton Mifflin Co., New York.

Otte, Daniel. 1981 and 1984. *North American Grasshoppers.* 2 volumes. Harvard University Press.

Pyle, Robert Michael. 1992. *Handbook for Butterfly Watchers.* Houghton Mifflin Co., Boston and New York.

Shaw, John. 1987. *John Shaw's Closeups in Nature: The Photographer's Guide to Techniques in the Field.* AMPHOTO, New York.

Usinger, Robert L., editor. 1956. *Aquatic Insects of California, With Keys to the North American Genera and Californian Species.* University of California Press, Berkeley and Los Angeles.

Walker, Edmund M. 1953 and 1958. *The Odonata of Canada and Alaska.* 2 volumes. The University of Toronto Press.

Walker, Edmund M., and Philip S. Corbet. 1975. *The Odonata of Canada and Alaska.* Volume 3. The University of Toronto Press.

Westfall, Minter J., Jr., and Michael L. May. 1996. *Damselflies of North America.* Scientific Publishers, Gainesville, Florida.

White, Richard E. 1983. *A Field Guide to the Beetles of North America.* Peterson Field Guide Series. Houghton Mifflin Co., New York.

Here is the contact information for various societies that can help you further your interest in bugs, and enhance your enjoyment of the subject. Some societies are local, and some are worldwide, but all have publications and meetings.

Societies

The Coleopterists' Society: contact the society's treasurer, currently Terry Seeno, CDFA-PPD, 3294 Meadowview Road, Sacramento, California, 95832-1448, U.S.A. e-mail: <tseeno@ns.net>.

Young Entomologists' Society: 1915 Peggy Place, Lansing, Michigan, U.S.A., 48910-2553. website: http://insects.ummz.lsa.umich.edu/yes/yes.html e-mail: <YESbugs@aol.com>.

Entomological Society of B.C.: Dr. Robb Bennett, Secretary Treasurer, B.C. Ministry of Forests, 7380 Puckle Road, Sannichton, B.C., V8M 1W4. website: http://www.harbour.com/commorgs/ESBC/about.html e-mail: <Robb.Bennett@gems6.gov.bc.ca>.

Entomological Society of Canada: 1320 Carling Avenue, Ottawa, Ontario, K1Z 7K9. website: http://www.biology.ualberta.ca/esc.hp/homepage.htm

Dragonfly Society of the Americas: c/o T. Donnelly, 2091 Partridge Lane, Binghamton, New York. 13903, U.S.A. website: http://www.afn.org/~iori/dsaintro.html

North American Butterfly Association: 4 Delaware Road, Morristown, New Jersey, 07960, U.S.A. website: http://www.naba.org

Lepidopterists' Society: c/o Los Angeles County Museum, 900 Exposition Boulevard, Los Angeles, California, 90007-4057, U.S.A. website: http://www.furman.edu/~snyder/snyder/lep/

And finally, for entomological supplies and/or books, contact:

Bio Quip Inc.: 17803 LaSalle Avenue, Gardena, California, U.S.A., 90248-3602. phone (310) 324 0620, fax (310) 324 7931, e-mail: <bioquip @aol.com>.

INDEX

Page numbers in **boldface** type refer to the primary, illustrated accounts.

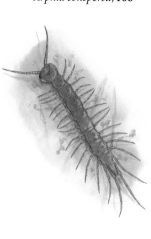

ABOUT THE AUTHOR

Since the age of five, John Acorn has been hopelessly fascinated by insects—a benign affliction that eventually led to a Master's degree in Entomology from the University of Alberta. His thesis work focused on tiger beetles, which are still among his favourite insects. Today, he works as an award-winning freelance writer, speaker and broadcaster, and he is best known as "Acorn, The Nature Nut," host of an international television series. He also is the co-author of *Birds of Coastal British Columbia*. John spends most of his spare time being exactly what you might expect—a bugster.

ABOUT THE ILLUSTRATOR

Ian Sheldon has been captivated by bugs since the age of three. Born in Edmonton, Ian later lived in South Africa, England and Singapore. Exposure to nature from so many different places enhanced his desire to study bugs further, and he earned an award from the Zoological Society of London and a degree from Cambridge University. He has also completed a Master's degree in Ecotourism Development, which involved research in Thailand. Ian is an award-winning artist represented by galleries internationally, and he is both a writer and illustrator of many other nature guides, including Lone Pine's *Seashore of British Columbia*.